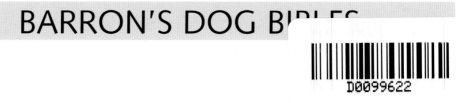

Yorkshire Terriers

D. Caroline Coile, Ph.D.

BARRON'S

Acknowledgments

Many Yorkshire Terrier owners throughout the years have helped greatly with educating me about all things Yorkie. Particular thanks are owed to Dr. Carolyn Hensley, Rae Tanner, Cindy Najara, and Dr. Carla Mayer.

About the Author

D. Caroline Coile, Ph.D. has written 30 books and more than 500 magazine and scientific articles about dogs—and one book about cats. She's also a columnist for *Dog World* magazine and the *AKC Gazette*. Her dog writing awards include the Dog Writer's Association of America Maxwell Award (seven times), Denlinger Award, the Eukanuba Canine Health Award (twice), and AKC Canine Health Foundation Award (twice). She is the author of the top selling *Barron's Encyclopedia of Dog Breeds*. Caroline's research and teaching interests revolve around canine behavior, senses, and genetics. On a practical level, Caroline has lived with dogs all of her life and competed with them for over 30 years. Her dogs have included nationally ranked show, field, obedience, and agility competitors, with Best in Show, Best in Field, and High in Trial (in both obedience and agility) awards.

All information and advice contained in this book has been reviewed by a veterinarian.

A Word About Pronouns

Many dog lovers feel that the pronoun "it" is not appropriate when referring to a pet that can be such a wonderful part of our lives. For this reason, Yorkshire Terriers are referred to as "he" in this book unless the topic specifically relates to female dogs. This by no means infers any preference, nor should it be taken as an indication that either sex is particularly problematic.

Photo Credits

Barbara Augello: pages 3, 32; Kent Dannen: pages 22, 148; Tara Darling: pages 5, 81, 170, 171; Jean Fogle: pages 12, 129; Isabelle Francais: pages 9, 27, 31, 35, 36, 46, 50, 55, 73, 90, 145, 146, 168; Shirley Fernandez/Paulette Johnson: pages 112, 123, 127; Daniel Johnson/Paulette Johnson: pages i, iii, v, 39, 57, 85, 93, 94, 96, 101, 104, 106, 134 (top and bottom), 135 (top and bottom), 136 (top and bottom), 137 (top and bottom), 138 (top and bottom), 139 (top and bottom), 140, 153, 159, 161, 162, 164, 178; Paulette Johnson: pages 15, 19, 20, 29, 45, 66, 119, 125, 167; Terri Lorbetske/Paulette Johnson: pages 43, 62, 109, 115, 143; Peter Rimsa: pages 57, 150; Pets by Paulette: pages 16, 60, 69, 71, 79, 92, 98, 160; Shutterstock: pages 40, 82, 87, 172, 174; Connie Summers/Paulette Johnson: pages vi, 6, 77.

Cover Credits

Front cover: Shutterstock; back cover: Tara Darling.

All inquiries should be addressed to:
Barron's Educational Series, Inc.
250 Wireless Boulevard
Hauppauge, New York 11788
www.barronseduc.com

ISBN-13: 978-0-7641-6254-1 (Book)
ISBN-10: 0-7641-6254-3 (Book)
ISBN-13: 978-0-7641-8678-3 (DVD)
ISBN-10: 0-7641-8678-7 (DVD)
ISBN-13: 978-0-7641-9652-2 (Package)
ISBN-10: 0-7641-9652-9 (Package)

Library of Congress Catalog Card No: 2009008922

Library of Congress Cataloging-in-Publication Data
Coile, D. Caroline.
    Yorkshire terriers / D. Caroline Coile.
        p. cm. — (Barron's dog bibles)
    Includes index.
    ISBN-13: 978-0-7641-6254-1
    ISBN-10: 0-7641-6254-3
    ISBN-13: 978-0-7641-8678-3
    ISBN-10: 0-7641-8678-7
    [etc.]
    1. Yorkshire terrier. I. Title.

    SF429.Y6C655 2009
    636.76—dc22
                                            2009008922

Printed in China

9 8 7 6 5 4

CONTENTS

CONTENTS

PREFACE

The Yorkshire Terrier is among the most glamorous of breeds. Arising from humble beginnings, he is as much at home in a celebrity's photo shoot as he is at a bedridden person's side. He can be seen co-piloting an 18-wheeler with his truck driver dad or frolicking at the seaside with the kids in his family. Sophisticated, cute, sweet, and sassy, the Yorkie, as his friends prefer to call him, is always full of surprises. Perhaps that's why he's risen to the place of second most popular dog in America.

The Yorkie is an accomplished lapdog, fun dog, therapy dog, and service dog. He's successful as a show dog, obedience dog, and agility dog, and even takes on tracking, Earthdog, and flyball. He is unrivaled as a companion.

He has special considerations, however. His tiny size makes him susceptible to some life-threatening problems that many owners don't know about. He has some hereditary health concerns. And he has a decided tendency to take over as boss of the house given half the chance.

In this book you'll learn about the Yorkie's past, what makes him tick, how to find a good one, how to raise and train your Yorkie, how to feed and groom him, and all the fun things you can do together. This book was written to help you be the best Yorkie owner you can be—and to help you make your Yorkie the best dog *he* can be—so you can share a long, happy life together.

Chapter One

All About Yorkshire Terriers

A sk ten Yorkie owners to tell you why Yorkies are the best dog breed and you'll get ten different answers: "loving," "sassy," "cute," "glamorous," "playful," "sweet," "big dog in a little body," and so on. Nobody can agree why, but enough people agree that Yorkies rule to make them the second most popular breed in America, and one of the most popular in the world. Few, however, realize the breed's modest start.

Birth of the Yorkshire Terrier

The Yorkshire Terrier's birthplace is Yorkshire, a huge county in northern England. It was an early center of woven textiles, specifically in towns such as Leeds, Huddersfield, Hull, and Sheffield. The industry attracted laborers who had previously worked on farms because textile work was steadier and the pay higher.

These laborers often brought their small terriers with them. Terriers were especially useful in urban situations because they could rid homes and mills of rats. The terrier's rat-killing ability also provided entertainment for the laborers. A tavern would set up a small pit, fill it with rats and a terrier, and take wagers on how many rats the dog could kill in a certain time.

By the late 1700s, a dog called the Waterside Terrier was well established in the region as a rat killer both along the docks and in the pits. It was a fairly small terrier weighing about 10 pounds, with a rough coat, often grayish in color.

Scottish laborers also migrated to the Yorkshire industrial towns, bringing with them other terriers, most notably the Roseneath Terrier from the Isle of Bute, and its probable descendents, the Skye, Paisley, and Clydesdale Terriers, collectively referred to as Scotch terriers (not to be confused with today's Scottish Terrier). They were all fairly small, from 10 to 16 pounds, with long or rough coats. In color, they were either solid fawn, solid gray, or blue and tan.

The Skye Terrier has been known at least since the sixteenth century. Skyes came in both harsh and silky coat types, both long. They were arbitrarily split into different breeds based on coat type and color, with the silky

1

all-blue ones becoming known as Paisley Terriers and the silky blue-and-tan ones as Clydesdale Terriers, both of which have since died out or merged with other breeds.

The Clydesdale was very likely the main breed that made up the Yorkshire Terrier. Comparisons of its early descriptions and points of the standard with those of the first Yorkshire Terrier standard reveal that the two breeds had much in common. But the Clydesdale wasn't the only breed to contribute to the Yorkshire Terrier gene pool. The Broken-Haired and Rough-Coated Toy Terrier also likely played a major role. Like the Clydesdale, these terriers had the tan pointed coat pattern along with the gene that gradually changes the coat from black to blue with age—the same gene responsible for the blue body coat of today's Yorkshire Terrier. Some also had silky coats, and most important, they were very small.

Breed Truths

Founding Fathers and Mothers

Three particular dogs had especially profound influence on establishing the Yorkshire Terrier. Although the exact crosses aren't known, they are believed to involve the following dogs:

• Swift's Old Crab, a crossbred Scotch terrier weighing about 9 pounds, with a long body and a coat of medium length. He had tan points.

• Kershaw's Kitty, either a Skye or Paisley Terrier with a long, solid-blue coat.

• An Old English Terrier of unknown name, with a grayish black coat and tan points.

Crab and Kitty were mated about six times, the last time in about 1850. The two produced 36 puppies, 28 of them males, which, in turn, sired many litters. Kitty later had 44 more puppies!

The Waterside Terrier (also called the Otter Terrier) probably played a role as well. One of the oldest types of terriers, the Waterside is described as early as the 1500s. Waterside Terriers came in black-and-tan and blue-and-tan coloring. The Old English Black and Tan Rough Coated Terrier is another possible contributor.

In 1859 an event happened that changed the Yorkshire Terrier from a "fancy terrier" ratter to a fancy terrier lapdog. In that year, the first dog show was held. It aroused so much interest that others followed, and demand for pure and exotic breeds ballooned. As the aristocracy, especially the ladies, became involved further demand for exotic lapdogs rose. This created great incentive for these dogs' working-class owners to create a fancy dog with long, silky hair and exotic coloring that would appeal to the wealthy.

In 1865, Huddersfield Ben, the dog known as the father of the modern Yorkshire Terrier, was born. He was one of the first Yorkshire Terriers to be shown, and he was very successful as both a show dog and a popular and prepotent stud. Despite dying young (he was killed by a carriage in 1871), he changed the look of the breed for decades to come.

During most of Ben's lifetime, he wasn't shown at England's official (English) Kennel Club shows, because the breed

was only admitted to official shows in 1870. Also during that time, there was no such breed as the Yorkshire Terrier. Instead, Ben and his kin were shown as Broken-Haired Scotch Terriers, or, sometimes, Toy Terriers or Blue Scotch Terriers, with several weight divisions ranging from under 4 pounds up to 12 pounds. Only in 1870 did a reporter covering a dog show suggest that they deserved a better name, suggesting, "Yorkshire Terrier" after the region in which they'd developed. The name caught on, and in 1874 England's Kennel Club officially listed the breed as Broken-Haired Scottish Terriers and Yorkshire Terriers. It was another twelve years, however, before the Kennel Club officially recognized the Yorkshire Terrier as a separate breed. The American Kennel Cub recognized them in 1885, not too long after the first Yorkies came to the New World.

Unlike many small dogs of the time, the Yorkie did not enjoy the favor of royalty. In the late 1800s and early 1900s, the fashion for lapdogs was round heads with very short muzzles, traits the Yorkie didn't share. It is true that it would have been fairly easy to breed these traits into the Yorkie, and the modern dogs are somewhat rounder of head and shorter of muzzle than the originals, but overall the Yorkie retained its more terrier-type head. It also remained in the shadows of popularity. Only in the 1960s did the breed begin to attract celebrity owners and be regarded as a status symbol. Of course, the masses followed, and thus began the Yorkie's steady climb toward the top of the popularity chart. They reached number two in 2006, and there's some speculation that the tiny Yorkie may end up in the number-one position eventually. Of course, anyone who knows a Yorkie knows that he is already number one in his own mind.

Yorkshire Terrier Timeline

Having trouble remembering the who, what, when, and where of Yorkie history? Here's a handy synopsis of Yorkie highlights over the years.

200 B.C.E. The earliest descriptions and fossil remains of terrier-like dogs come from around this time in Europe. The Romans call dogs that followed quarry underground *terraii*, from the Latin *"terra,"* for "earth."

1000s: The first of the Forest Laws, which eventually govern as much as one third of English lands, are enacted to protect royal game animals in royal lands. These laws forbid serfs from owning dogs capable of hunting large game. One requirement is that any of their dogs have to be small enough to pass through a 7-inch hoop. Terriers flourish because they are small enough to pass the hoop test and to be secreted for poaching, yet tough and quick enough to dispatch vermin and small game. The Forest Laws were abandoned in the 1700s.

Circa 1500: The earliest picture of any terrier in England appears in the illuminated manuscript "Hours of the Virgin." It depicts a small black and tan terrier, which is identified as a Waterside Terrier.

1700s: The Industrial Revolution begins in England with emphasis on textile mills. Farm workers move from the country to cities, bringing with them the terriers they had used to keep rats down in their barns and houses.

Circa 1850: Crosses create the dogs that will become the first Yorkshire Terriers.

1859: The first dog show is held in England, creating interest in fancy dogs.

1865: Huddersfield Ben, called the father of the breed, is born.

1866: The first of the breed are shown as Broken-Haired Terriers.

1870: The name "Yorkshire Terrier" is accepted.

1886: England's Kennel Club officially recognizes the Yorkshire Terrier as a separate breed.

1872: The first Yorkshire Terrier, a dog named Punch, is recorded in Australia. He is closely related to Huddersfield Ben.

1872: The first recorded birth of a Yorkshire Terrier in America is a dog named Jack.

1878: Separate classes are first offered for Yorkshire Terriers at American dog shows. The first Yorkies are also shown at the Westminster Kennel Club Dog Show.

1885: The Yorkshire Terrier is admitted into the American Kennel Club studbook.

1888: The first Yorkshire Terrier is registered in Canada.

1890: The first American Champion is recorded, a dog named Bradford Harry.

1893: The first Yorkshire Terrier is registered in Mexico.

1897: The first Yorkshire Terrier English Champions are recorded: the male, Merry Mentor, and the female, Ashton Queen.

1898: The first Yorkshire Terrier breed club in England, as well as in the world, is formed.

1900: The American Kennel Club (AKC) registers a total of 11 new Yorkshire Terriers.

1909: The AKC registers a total of 30 new Yorkshire Terriers.

1913: The first attempt to form the Yorkshire Terrier Club of America is made. It folds after several years.

1919: The Yorkshire Terrier Association of America is formed. It folds after five years.

1937: Another attempt to form the Yorkshire Terrier Club of America is made. It folds with the onset of World War II.

1938: The Yorkshire Terrier wins the Toy Group for the first time at the Westminster Kennel Club Dog Show. The winner is Champion Miss Wynsum.

1939: The AKC registers a total of 69 new Yorkshire Terriers.

1940: The AKC registers a total of 91 new Yorkshire Terriers.

1943: The AKC registers a total of 33 new Yorkshire Terriers, the numbers down because of World War II.

1944: Smoky, a Yorkshire Terrier, is found in a foxhole and goes on to become a war hero. When she comes to America after the war, she is treated like a celebrity. Her appearances on television and in print do much to make the breed known.

1949: The AKC registers a total of 173 new Yorkshire Terriers.

1951: The first AKC Best in Show to be won by a Yorkie occurs. The dog is Ch Little Sir Model.

1956: The United Kennel Club (UKC), the second-largest dog registry in the United States, recognizes the Yorkshire Terrier.

1958: The Yorkshire Terrier Club of America becomes the official AKC parent club for the breed.

1960s: The Yorkshire Terrier begins to climb significantly in popularity. More than 1,000 are AKC registered in 1960.

1970s: The Yorkshire Terrier is the most popular breed in Britain. In America, more than 13,000 are registered in one year.

1980: Almost 25,000 Yorkshire Terriers are registered in America.

1995: The Yorkshire Terrier becomes one of the ten most popular breeds in America, with almost 37,000 new registrations.

2006: The Yorkshire Terrier becomes the second most popular breed in America, with more than 48,000 registered. It is the fifteenth most popular breed in England.

Yorkies by the Pound

The first Yorkshire Terriers were larger dogs, weighing in the teens, but very early on in their history there were dogs weighing less than 8 pounds. Yorkshire Terriers are currently rivaled only by Chihuahuas in the quest for recognition as the world's smallest breed. In fact, the all-time record for smallest dog is held by a Yorkshire Terrier named Sylvia, who weighed 4 ounces and measured 2.8 inches tall at the shoulder.

The *Guinness Book of World Records* listed a Yorkie from Thailand named Big Boss as the smallest dog from 1995 to 2002. Big Boss was 4.7 inches tall. Before 1995, the record was held by a Yorkie named Thumbelina, who measured 5.5 inches tall. After Big Boss, the record was held by a Yorkie

named Whitney, who measured only
3 inches tall.

In terms of length, the title of world's
smallest was once held by a Yorkie named
Tiny Pinocchio, who measured 8 inches
long and 4.75 inches tall. He weighed
one pound and slept in a birdcage for his
own safety.

Yorkies in the Public Eye

Yorkies have been in the public eye since
they first appeared by the sides of upper-
class ladies. The image of Yorkies as pres-
tige symbols has persisted through the
years by way of a variety of mediums.

In art, Yorkshire Terriers appear in fine
oil paintings of the late nineteenth century
by such artists as William Luker, Ernest
Girardot, and Carl Suhrlandt, and in the
early twentieth century in the work of the
noted dog artist Maud Earl.

Yorkies have appeared on the big screen
in *Funny Face* (which featured Audrey
Hepburn's own Yorkie, Mr. Famous), *Meet
the Fockers*, *Urban Legend*, *Daltry Calhoun*,
A Fish Called Wanda, *High School Musical 2*,
and *Shall We Dance*?

On television, perhaps the most remem-
bered Yorkie was Mignon on *Green Acres*.
Other shows with Yorkies include *Lou
Grant*, *Being Bobby Brown*, *The George Carlin
Show*, *'Til Death Do Us Part: Carmen and Dave*, and *Groomer Has It*.

In literature, the Yorkie has not been as well represented. One appears in
the Fred Basset comic strip. And many people believe that the original Toto
in *The Wonderful Wizard of Oz* was a Yorkshire Terrier, judging from the
book's illustrations.

Five Famous Yorkies

Today's Yorkie popularity stems primarily from word-of-mouth and eye-
witness accounts of the everday fun and companionship they provide. But a
few Yorkies have pushed the breed's popularity by appealing to the masses.
Following are the five most influential Yorkies.

BE PREPARED! What a Yorkshire Terrier Will Cost

Purchase: $250–$1800 ($50–$250 for a dog from a shelter or rescue group)

Spaying or neutering: $35–$200. Spaying costs more than neutering, and both cost more for larger dogs. Some communities offer low-cost spay-neuter clinics. The fee may be especially low if you have adopted your puppy from a shelter.

Vaccinations: $25–$75 per visit, with three visits typical in the first year. If you buy an older puppy, he may already have some or all of his vaccinations. As an adult, he may only need vaccinations every three years, but he should still have a yearly checkup. Some cities have low-cost clinics that provide basic services such as vaccinations at a lower fee. Ask at your local shelter.

Worming: $20–$30 per episode. Most puppies need to be wormed several times. Worming medications are dosed by weight, so Yorkies have an advantage here. Tapeworm medication is most expensive.

Heartworm prevention: $4–$6 per month. In most parts of the country, you'll need to start your puppy on heartworm prevention. The preventive is by weight and is given once a month.

Flea prevention: $8–$12 a month. In most parts of the country, you'll need to start flea prevention right away.

Accidents and illnesses: $100–$200 and up per minor illness or accident. Surgery to correct a portosystemic shunt typically costs between $1,500 and $4,000. Surgery to correct luxating patellas typically costs $1,200 to $2,400.

Food: $15–$20 per month. Dry food costs less than canned food.

Accessories: $20–$100. Collars, leashes, toys, crates, dog beds, cute outfits, carrying bags—you can spend as much as you want.

Boarding: $15–$40 per day. Additional services, such as grooming, walking, or training, cost extra.

Obedience classes: $50–$150 per 8-week session. Private lessons cost more. Lessons offered by a dog or obedience club usually cost less.

Grooming: $40-$100 per month. Cut costs by having your veterinarian show you how to clip nails, and buy a nail clipper to do it yourself. Keep your dog tangle-free, since groomers charge extra for matted dogs.

Health insurance: $0 to $400 for the first year. Different policies have different deductibles and coverage. Insurance is a good option for accident-prone pets. Some people instead put away money in account earmarked for veterinary emergencies.

License: $0-$60 per year. Most urban areas require annual licenses for dogs, although many rural areas do not. The fee for spayed and neutered dogs is often less than that for intact dogs.

Fence or containment: $200-$2000 and up. The best containment system is a fence, but you can also have a kennel run. The fence should be secure enough to keep other dogs out.

Home repair: $15 and up. Chewed furniture, shredded carpet, new paint for doors, and screens for windows are the most common projects.

Note: Costs in metropolitan areas tend to be higher than costs in rural areas.

Huddersfield Ben, father of the breed. Born in 1865 in Huddersfield, England, Ben was both an accomplished ratter and a show dog. He won more than 70 prizes at dog shows and was a sought-after stud, consistently siring small true-to-type Yorkies that established the look of the breed. Every Yorkshire Terrier today descends from him, mostly through ten of his sons and one daughter. Ben was killed in a street accident at six years of age.

"Corporal" Smoky, war hero. Found in a New Guinea jungle foxhole during World War II, 4-pound Smoky was bought for the equivalent of $6.44. She then accompanied her owner on twelve missions in the Pacific over an 18-month period. She became a hero when a wire had to be run through an 8-inch culvert under a runway to make the airstrip operational. Guided by her owner's calls on the other end, Smoky squeezed through the 70-foot-long culvert with the wire attached to her, dragging it behind her. After the war she became a television personality, appearing on live TV for 42 weeks without repeating a trick. She is considered to be the first therapy dog on record, as she visited wounded troops over a period of 12 years. Smoky popularized the Yorkshire Terrier more than any other dog. A book, *Yorkie Doodle Dandy*, was written about her exploits.

Sylvia, bonsai bowser. The smallest recorded dog ever was a Yorkshire Terrier in England named Sylvia, who as an adult reportedly weighed only 4 ounces, stood 2.8 inches tall at the shoulder, and measured 3.5 inches from the tip of her nose to tail. She died in 1945, when she was not quite two years old.

Champion Cede Higgins, Westminster winner. The Westminster Kennel Club Dog Show is second only to the Kentucky Derby as the longest continually running sporting event in America. But in all the years since its inception in 1877, only once has the Best in Show nod gone to a Yorkshire Terrier, in 1978. It was Higgins' thirty-third Best in Show, and the one that made history.

Champion Ozmilion Mystification, Crufts conqueror. The Crufts dog show in England is the largest annual dog show in the world, as prestigious in Europe as Westminster is in America. Justin, as Ozmilion Mystification was known, won Best in Show at Crufts in 1997, when he was five years old. The previous year he was the top show dog of all breeds in England.

Yorkshire Terrier Health

Yorkshire Terriers are long-lived dogs, typically living well into their teens. Like every breed of dog, the Yorkshire Terrier has a closed gene pool, which increases the possibility that dogs possessing the same recessive genes for a particular hereditary disease will breed with one another. The less related two dogs are, the lower this possibility, which is why, when you select a puppy, you should look at the pedigree and avoid highly inbred litters (ones in which the sire and dam are related).

Most Yorkies are fairly healthy, but the breed is susceptible to several health problems.

Portosystemic shunt: Also called portocaval or liver shunt, this condition is more common in Yorkshire Terriers than in any other breed. It occurs when part of the vein that normally takes blood to the liver for cleansing bypasses the liver, so some blood continues to circulate without being rid of normal waste products such as waste. The waste builds up and can cause stunted growth and neurological problems, sometimes starting in puppyhood. Affected dogs may need surgery to correct the condition or a special diet to live with it. See page 102 for more information.

Patellar luxation: Also known as slipping kneecaps, this is a fairly common condition in most small dogs. It occurs when the kneecap isn't held in its proper place at the front of the knee joint, but instead slips in and out. It can be mild or severe; if severe, the dog will need surgery to properly walk and run. See page 91 for more information.

Portosystemic shunt and patellar luxation are the two most widespread serious conditions that affect Yorkies, and probably the only two that would affect a person's decision to choose a Yorkie versus another breed that may or may not share the same health concerns. Other conditions that appear at higher-than-normal rates are tracheal collapse (causing breathing problems), Legg-Calvé-Perthes disease (a hip problem), hydrocephalus ("water on the brain"), patent ductus arteriosis (a congenital heart disease), and progressive retinal atrophy (a hereditary eye disease). These are discussed in greater detail in Chapter Six.

Chapter Two

The Mind of the Yorkshire Terrier

When you consider adding a Yorkie to your life, only do so with the intention of getting him for keeps. A dog isn't a trial-run item, or a passing interest, but a sentient being who won't understand why he's been relegated to the garage or backyard or taken to the animal shelter. Shelters are full of dogs, even Yorkies, that were once welcomed into homes with excitement, but unfortunately, often without preparation or commitment. Yorkies are the second most popular breed in America—yet they aren't for everyone.

The World According to Yorkies

Yorkies' outlook on life is simple: The world exists for them. People, beds, laps, treats, cars, designer bags, parades, parties—all are put on earth exclusively for their pleasure and entertainment. They expect to be doted on, and most Yorkie owners are glad to oblige.

Your Yorkie will not live his life awaiting your next command, but if you make doing your bidding worthwhile, he can learn quickly and, in fact, greatly enjoys showing off what he knows. He'd prefer, however, that you do *his* bidding, and he will make your obedience worth your while by rewarding you with generous kisses and tail wags.

Although very adaptable to apartment living, he harbors an inner wolf, or at least an inner terrier, and likes nothing more than to explore the outdoors. His independent and adventurous streak make this a chancy proposition unless he's well trained to come when called and you know ahead of time he cannot roam too far, even if he does take off in hot pursuit of a butterfly—or grizzly bear. In his mind, he can take on either one.

The Yorkshire Terrier is one of the most popular breeds in the world. No doubt this is partly because of his stunning and glamorous coat, which he wears like a royal cape. But most pet owners choose to keep their Yorkies in cute short clips, so the coat can't explain the breed's real appeal. Yorkies seem to have something for everyone. They are docile and loving lapdogs

BE PREPARED! Are You Ready for a Yorkie?

Before you get a Yorkshire Terrier, make sure you're ready for a dog in general and a Yorkie in particular.

1. Do you plan to keep this dog his entire life, anticipated to be 12 to 16 years?

2. Is your future settled enough that you won't find yourself having to move to a place that doesn't accept dogs?

3. Does everyone in the family want a dog? This is especially vital if the dog is going to interfere with the family's vacation plans or other activities.

4. Who will care for the dog? This person must really want a dog, not just be agreeing without thinking it through. This person must be an adult.

5. How old are your children? Experts recommend waiting until your children are at least 6 years old before bringing in a puppy.

6. Is anybody in the house allergic to dogs? Before you get a dog, spend some time around other households with dogs, especially Yorkies, to make sure nobody is allergic, or that allergies are not too uncomfortable.

7. Where will the dog live? Dogs make better family members and companions when they live with the family in the home. Dogs are social animals and will be very unhappy if forced to live by themselves.

8. Are you home enough to care for a dog? You don't have to be a stay-at-home doggy parent, but if your dog is going to be alone for 12-hour stretches, you're not in a position to care for him.

9. Do you have a fenced yard? While not totally necessary for a Yorkie if you use indoor pads (see page 51) or live in an apartment, a secure yard makes caring for a dog a lot easier, as you won't always have to walk him at inopportune times.

10. Do you plan to train your dog? Training not only teaches your dog vital manners that make him easier to live with, but the act of training, when done properly, reinforces bonding.

11. Are you somebody who cannot tolerate mess or some damage to your belongings? Then don't get a dog. No matter how careful you are, something will get chewed up or wet on.

12. Does barking drive you crazy? Yorkies bark. You can train them to bark less, but barking is part of their nature.

13. Do you expect strict obedience? Then don't get a Yorkie!

14. Do you want a dog that gazes at you adoringly all day long? Better keep some treats in your pocket then, or get a different breed.

15. Do you want a dog that will cuddle with you and play with you equally enthusiastically? Then get a Yorkie!

for the elderly, energetic playmates for children, and even tenacious tough guys for men. They can snuggle and love or play and explore. Even so, they're not the perfect match for everyone, and like all breeds, they have their pros and cons.

Yorkshire Terrier Pros and Cons

Yorkie good points are obvious. Their small size makes them easy and affordable to keep and maintain. Their striking coat and cute appearance make them the subject of attention. They enjoy both cuddling on a lap and playing a rambunctious game. They are very bright and quick to learn, and enjoy doing tricks. They can bring a smile to anyone's lips!

But Yorkies aren't for everyone. They're somewhat independent and may not always listen to you if something more interesting beckons. They can be stubborn, especially if you try to win a battle of the wills. They are natural watchdogs, and tend to bark a lot. They have extremely active minds and need to challenge their intellect every day; otherwise, they can channel their inquisitive nature into getting in trouble.

COMPATIBILITY Is a Yorkie the Best Breed for You?

ENERGY LEVEL	● ● ● ●
EXERCISE REQUIREMENTS	●
PLAYFULNESS	● ● ● ●
AFFECTION LEVEL	● ● ●
FRIENDLINESS TOWARD OTHER PETS	● ●
FRIENDLINESS TOWARD STRANGERS	● ● ●
FRIENDLINESS TOWARD CHILDREN	● ● ●
EASE OF TRAINING	● ●
HOUSETRAINING EASE	● ●
BARKING	● ● ● ●
GROOMING REQUIREMENTS	● ● ● ●
SHEDDING	●
SPACE REQUIREMENTS	●
OK FOR BEGINNERS	● ● ●

4 Dots = Highest rating on scale

The Yorkie's size can be a problem. They can be easily injured by rough play with children, by an adult tripping over them, or by a large dog. They can even be injured from falling fruit outdoors! As puppies, they need extra vigilance to make sure they eat regularly and don't develop hypoglycemia (page 61).

Coat care requires a commitment, especially if you plan to let it grow long. Long hair needs to be brushed or combed every day or two. Short hair doesn't need as much daily care, but needs clipping every 4 to 6 weeks.

Breed Truths

Yorkshire Terrier Personality

- Bold
- Independent
- Affectionate
- Playful
- Clever
- Loving
- Energetic
- Watchful
- Territorial
- Gregarious
- Humorous

Like many toy breeds, Yorkies are difficult to housetrain. In fact, lack of housetraining is one of the most commonly cited reasons for giving a Yorkie up to rescue. Males seem to be a little more difficult than females. Housetraining is something you must be serious about right from the start.

Yorkies can also bark a lot. This makes them great watchdogs, but if you live in an apartment, it may not make you a popular neighbor. Barking is the other most commonly cited problem behavior for giving up a Yorkie.

Yorkies tend to have some costly health problems, most notably portosystemic shunt and patellar luxation. Read the section on hereditary health problems before choosing your dog.

Yorkie Caveats

1. If ever a dog was born with a gold crown on its head, it's the Yorkshire Terrier. It doesn't take long before the typical Yorkie decides you exist to wait on him and fulfill his every wish. While in truth part of the fun in having a Yorkie is being able to treat him like royalty, you have to be careful lest you create a little tyrant. Yorkies have a knack for picking out who is likely to succumb to their demands, and they don't hesitate to take advantage. A spoiled Yorkie can become so overbearing that he doesn't let his people sit on the sofa next to him or even get in the bed when he's in it. So Yorkie caveat #1 is that they have a tendency to abuse their power.

2. Many Yorkies carry that king complex with them when they meet other dogs. They have a tendency to forget their size, or to overestimate it tremendously; it's not uncommon for one to blaze up to a big dog and dare it to try something. The problem is that when big dogs go ahead and try something, it doesn't take much for them to seriously injure even the toughest Yorkie.

3. Despite their baby-doll looks, Yorkies are terriers at heart. Don't be surprised if your picture of innocence pops up with a mouse in his mouth or takes off in the park after a rabbit. He has generations of scrappy hunters behind him, and what self-respecting terrier could pass up the

chance to raise some havoc? If your Yorkie kills a pet rat, it's going to be your fault for leaving them together unsupervised.

4. Yorkies are fun to carry, and often it's safest and easiest to carry your dog. But some Yorkies come to enjoy their life of leisure so much that they protest when actually asked to use their own four legs. Don't become your Yorkie's beast of burden.

Fashion Yorkies?

One of the perks of owning a tiny dog is the ability to take him with you almost anywhere by means of a doggy carrier that looks like a purse. Done responsibly, that's a great idea. But as much as dogs like to go with you, sitting in a doggie purse all day isn't that much fun, and it doesn't give your dog that much exercise. So don't overdo it.

Some people get a Yorkie and a doggie purse for the wrong reason. They see the many celebrities with their Yorkies in tow and think a Yorkie makes the ideal fashion accessory. It doesn't. Unlike other accessories, a dog can't be put in the closet or chest when you get home, and you don't get rid of him when the styles change. Yorkies are dogs, not accessories!

CAUTION

Three Reasons NOT to Buy Your Child a Yorkie

1. Don't buy a Yorkie as a way to teach a child responsibility. Children seldom live up to their promises of feeding and walking the dog. It's unfair to let the dog suffer in order to teach the child a lesson. In almost every family, a parent ends up taking care of the dog.

2. Don't buy a Yorkie because your child decides one day that he wants one. This is a decision for the entire family, and especially the person who will be in charge of caring for the dog. A week from now the child may not even remember the dog he absolutely had to have.

3. Don't buy a Yorkie, or any dog, as a desperate last-minute holiday gift. Dogs are not impulse items. A puppy shouldn't have to compete with all the other gifts on special occasions. If, however, the entire family is sold on the idea, you can gift wrap a leash, bowl, or video of your puppy-to-come, and place them under the Christmas tree.

Yorkies and Children

A child and a Yorkshire Terrier can form a friendship that will last well into your child's teens, and one that may be as close as that of siblings. Don't be surprised if your Yorkie consistently chooses your child's bed over yours, or prefers her company. Kids are fun! Kids and Yorkies share a sense of playfulness and adventure—and mischief!

Yorkies aren't a good match for very young children, however, because until children learn to control how roughly they play, they can hurt such a small animal. Teach children to play with the dog on the floor so they can neither fall on nor drop the dog.

Young children should never be given the responsibility of walking the dog alone. It's too easy for the dog to get away, or for another dog to attack, and children aren't equipped to handle such emergencies. Not only could the Yorkie be hurt, but the child may be inclined to do heroic, but foolish, things to save her dog.

Yorkies and Other Pets

Yorkies generally get along well with other household pets. Occasionally two Yorkies of the same sex will decide there's not room for the two of them, but that's the exception rather than the rule. Most Yorkies get along well with the family cat, and can even become close friends. Because of their terrier heritage, don't trust a Yorkie to ignore any pet rodents.

Chapter Three

How to Choose a Yorkshire Terrier

"You get what you pay for" is only partly true when it comes to adding a new dog to your family. Many people have found wonderful Yorkie companions at bargain prices, or even for free, and too many others have paid exorbitant prices for Yorkies with poor conformation, health, and temperament. As long as your dog looks like a Yorkie, perfect conformation may not be that important to you, but good health and good temperament are vital to any dog. Good breeders place health and temperament foremost when deciding if they should breed a litter.

The Best Sources

Your best chance of getting a good Yorkie is to find a breeder who is careful about the dogs he or she breeds, the way they are raised, and the homes they go to. Besides being your best source of a puppy with good health, good temperament, and good looks, a good breeder will be a mentor and friend. You will always be able to ask questions, share anecdotes, and find help. You will find yourself part of an extended family of puppy owners, and you can keep up with littermates throughout their lives. Should circumstances arise that force you to surrender your dog, good breeders are there to make sure he is taken care of.

Some of the best breeders are those who make Yorkie breeding their life's love. They may breed for show or obedience competition. Such breeders produce only a few litters a year, with the goal being to improve their lines. Not every puppy will be a great show dog, however, and these puppies are sold as pets. They will have received the same care as the breeder's next champion prospects, and they are usually sold for affordable prices if your home is deemed appropriate. Good breeders are happy to talk Yorkie with you, and won't hesitate to talk you out of getting a Yorkie from them if they feel the breed isn't the best match for you. One way to evaluate breeders is to compare how they evaluate you. Good breeders are choosy about where their puppies go. They make sure their puppies go to homes where they will be loved for a lifetime. Good breeders will ask about your experience with

dogs, and with small dogs and Yorkies in particular. They will ask about your facilities and family. They will discuss expenses, training, grooming, health care, and safety issues with you. They may require that you neuter or spay your dog. They may ask you to wait for several months for a puppy; during this "cooling off" period they can make sure you are not just impulse buying. If a breeder doesn't care where her puppies are going, she probably doesn't care where they came from either, and there's a good chance very little thought went into breeding and raising the litter. The best place to find conscientious breeders is through Yorkshire Terrier clubs and shows, or the Yorkshire Terrier Club of America (YTCA).

YTCA Member Breeders

The Yorkshire Terrier Club of America breeder list, available online at *www.ytca.org/breeder1.html*, is a good place to find responsible breeders. These breeders are all members of the YTCA and have agreed to abide by its code of ethics (*http://ytca.org/ethics.html*). Although the code is not enforceable, its principles reflect a standard that all breeders should uphold.

Among the items mentioned in the YTCA Code of Ethics are that each breeder should devote herself to the betterment of the breed; keep accurate records of all breedings and registrations; sell with a contract that ensures the breeder is contacted should the owner not be able to keep the dog, and assist in the placement of that dog; sell pet-quality dogs with neuter/spay contracts; sell dogs with written bills of sale detailing registration information, pedigree, medical history, terms of sale, and instructions for feeding and care; and not allow dogs to go to their new homes until 12 weeks of age.

Clubs and Shows

Local Yorkshire Terrier clubs (*www.ytca.org/regionalclubs.html*) can also be a valuable source of information about upcoming litters and events. Having a local breeder is a great advantage because you can get to know the breeder and her dogs firsthand, and she also can get to know you. Having your breeder close by is especially helpful for training advice and just for having an extended Yorkie family.

A great way to meet breeders and see lots of Yorkies is to attend a dog show, especially a Yorkshire Terrier specialty show. A specialty show is a prestigious event that attracts Yorkies from far away. A list of upcoming specialties can be found at *www.ytca.org/calendar.html*.

If no local Yorkie clubs or specialties are nearby, you may be able to find an all-breed club by going to *www.akc.org*, and clicking on Clubs, then Club Search. You can join a local club or simply attend a local all-breed dog show. (Find these by going to www.akc.org, and clicking on Events, then Event and Awards Search). The premier Yorkshire Terrier show is the national specialty show, held in New York City each winter just before the Westminster Kennel Club show. In addition, a second YTCA specialty is held in a different part of the country each year. To find the date and location, go to *www.ytca.org*.

Magazines and Internet Research

You can also find good breeders in Yorkshire Terrier and all-breed dog magazines. Or join one of the many online Yorkie discussion lists and get to know breeders there. Try to find a group that has interests in various dog competitions and activities, rather than ones populated only by pet owners comparing cute stories—although those are worth joining for fun!

Avoid breeders who:

- advertise teacup, doll-face, or exotic-colored Yorkies.
- are unaware of, or don't acknowledge, Yorkie health problems such as patellar luxation, portosystemic (liver) shunts, tracheal collapse, patent ductus arteriosis (a malformation of the heart), Legg-Calvé-Perthes disease, or urinary stones.
- are willing to send a puppy home before the age of 10 weeks (twelve weeks is preferable).
- sell through third-party brokers so you can't talk to the actual breeders.

The Best Age

Most responsible Yorkie breeders keep their puppies to 12 weeks of age before allowing them to go to their new homes. In fact, the YTCA Code of Conduct states: "All puppies leaving the breeder's possession will be a minimum of 12 weeks of age to facilitate adequate socialization as well as appropriate emotional and temperament development through interaction with siblings, dam, and other dogs." This is considerably older than the 8 weeks that breeders of

BE PREPARED! 10 Questions to Ask Breeders

1. **Do you specialize in Yorkshire Terriers?** Good breeders work with only one or two breeds of dogs, so they can concentrate on just those breeds. Breeders with a smorgasbord of breeds and crossbreeds tend to be in the business of producing puppies for profit, and may not be as selective in choosing parents.

2. **Do you have litters available all the time?** Good breeders seldom have puppies available immediately and will ask to put you on a waiting list. That's because they don't breed a lot, and their dogs are in demand. They may have dogs they have chosen not to breed because, in the breeder's opinion, those dogs may not produce good puppies.

3. **Can I visit or see a video of the puppies in their environment?** Good breeders are proud of their dogs and facilities. It used to be that a home visit was a necessity, but because of safety issues, more breeders are wary about inviting relative strangers into their home. But you should be able to see pictures or a video of the puppies in their environment.

4. **Can I meet the dam or see a video of the dam?** Good breeders have the dam available. The sire, however, may live elsewhere. Again, at the very least, photos, and preferably videos, of both sire and dam should be available.

5. **How did you choose these parents?** Good breeders should be able to discuss the merits and possible shortcomings of both parents, and why they chose to breed them.

6. **Can I see the pedigree?** Good breeders have the pedigree on hand, without searching or sending for it. In fact, good breeders will also have pictures and knowledge of many of the dogs in the pedigree for several generations back.

7. **Are the puppies registered?** Good breeders will have AKC-registered dogs (or their dogs will be registered with the national kennel club in whatever country they're in). The United Kennel Club is the only other acceptable registry in the United States.

8. **Is there a written sales agreement?** Good breeders will supply a written agreement that includes the registration information, price, and any conditions.

9. **Is there a health warranty?** Good breeders will warranty the puppy's health, barring accident, for about a week after you've taken possession and under certain conditions. They will not, however, warranty it for years, because nobody can make such a promise. As with all living beings, dogs can become prematurely ill, and can suffer from unforeseen hereditary problems. At this time, no DNA tests exist for the most common Yorkie hereditary health problems, but choosing a litter from a family in which such problems seldom occur is a good start.

10. **What do you need from me?** Good breeders ask for more than money. In fact, that's the last thing they mention. They want evidence that you're going to provide a good home for their puppies for life.

larger dogs use as the age of placement. But because of their tiny size, Yorkie puppies need considerably more care than larger dogs. This is mostly because of a potentially fatal condition called hypoglycemia (page 61), which can strike young Yorkies and other tiny puppies when stressed or hungry.

The period between 7 and 12 weeks is also crucial for socialization and learning new experiences, which means your breeder will have to undertake this big responsibility. If your breeder is unwilling to do so, she may not be the breeder you want. Don't worry that an older Yorkie, even an adult, won't accept you as part of his family; as long as you love him and interact with him, and if he was well socialized, he will meld into your life and family as though he were born there.

Rescue

Homeless Yorkies may find their way to rescue organizations, which are groups that take in dogs, usually of a particular breed, to find homes for them. Homeless Yorkies are more common than you might think. They can become homeless for many reasons. Sometimes their families simply can't keep them, and sometimes their families don't want to make the effort to keep them. Sometimes the Yorkie barks too much, jumps up too much, destroys too much, or relieves himself on the rug too much. Most of these problems can be corrected or improved, but many people either never try or try the wrong way. Sometimes the Yorkie gets old or develops a health problem and is suddenly seen as a burden. Rescue Yorkies come in all ages, although puppies are in the minority. Many rescues have been cherished companions and are suddenly alone in the world. Other rescues may be discarded puppy mill producers who have lived out their reproductive usefulness. Some rescues have never lived in a house before, or known a gentle touch or kind word. With time, training, and security they gradually adapt to their new circumstances and become exceptional family companions.

Many rescue groups provide temperament testing, basic training, and behavior consultation. Adopting from a rescue group provides new owners

Helpful Hints

Rescue Resources

Adopt-a-Yorkie:
http://adopt-a-yorkie.adoptapet.com

Canadian Yorkshire Terrier Rescue:
www.canadianyorkshireterrierrescue.com

Petfinders: *www.petfinders.com*

Rescue Me Yorkie Rescue:
www.yorkierescueme.com

Save a Yorkie Rescue:
www.saveayorkierescue.org

Save Our Small Dogs:
www.sosdogs.org

United Yorkie Rescue:
www.unitedyorkierescue.org

Yorkie Haven Rescue:
www.yorkiehavenrescue.com

Yorkshire Terrier National Rescue:
www.ytnr.com

YTCA Rescue:
www.ytca.org/mainview.htm

with a safety net should problems arise. Many groups require adoptive owners to enroll in obedience classes in order to encourage bonding, basic dog training skills, and basic manners. They also often provide opportunities to become club members, participate in Yorkie activities and rescue reunions, and even become part of the rescue team.

Rescue groups need to charge a reasonable fee in order to recoup their expenses and continue to provide services. Some rescue dogs are less expensive than others, however. Generally, a Yorkie from a county shelter is the least expensive, while those from Yorkie rescue groups cost more. Dogs from the latter, however, are usually examined for health and temperament problems, and treated as needed, so that the costs even out. Regardless, a rescue Yorkie is the deal of a lifetime.

Puppy Size

Yorkshire Terriers are one of the smallest breeds of dogs, yet some breeders try to sell "teacup" Yorkies. The YTCA Code of Ethics states that breeders should not use the terms "teacup," "tiny specialists," or similar wording in advertising. No separate teacup type of Yorkie exists, although some Yorkies are certainly smaller than others. As appealing as it may seem to have the smallest dog around, extra-small Yorkies have some drawbacks, especially for owners not already experienced with tiny dog care. Their small size makes them more vulnerable to accidents and injuries. They are less safe around other dogs and small children. They can even be carried away by birds of prey! Although they may be easier to carry in a doggy purse, they may be more difficult to take walking in tall grass. In fact, if you are considering partaking in any dog competitions, a larger Yorkie will have a much easier time at outdoor events. A larger female Yorkie is also a safer choice if you plan to breed. Smaller Yorkies are more prone to hypoglycemia (page 61), and require much more care as puppies in order to prevent it. They are also more likely to have a molera (page 31), hydrocephalus (page 89), and tooth loss. See the chart on page 59 to predict adult weight from puppy weight.

Fun Facts

Litter Size

Yorkies typically have litters of from two to four puppies. The record is eight puppies, whelped in 2008 by a 7-pound Yorkie named Kingcreek's London Fog. She almost doubled her weight during her pregnancy. She delivered the puppies by natural birth, trumping the previous eight-puppy Yorkie litter delivered by Caesarean.

Doll-Faced Yorkies

Although it seems like all Yorkies have cute baby-doll faces, the term "doll-face" is used for those that have shorter muzzles and rounder heads than the ideal Yorkshire Terrier called for in the standard. The YTCA Code of Ethics states that breeders should not use the term "doll-face" or similar

terms (such as "baby doll" or "apple headed") in advertising. Not only are such heads not what the standard calls for, but tiny dogs with round heads are more likely to have hydrocephalus or moleras.

Puppy Coat Color and Texture

Some breeders offer Yorkies in so-called exotic colors that are not true Yorkie colors. These include spotted dogs (parti-colors), solid-colored dogs (with no tan points), and chocolate-colored dogs (rather than steel-blue color on the body coat). The AKC Yorkshire Terrier standard disqualifies Yorkies with solid-colored coats, or any combination of colors other than blue and tan as described in the standard, and any dogs with white markings other than a small white spot on the forechest that cannot be more than one inch in diameter in any direction. While dogs with these disqualifications make beautiful companions, you should be aware that they are considered faults, not attributes.

Yorkie puppy coats can be confusing. Although the adults have long, silky hair that should be a metallic blue on the body with clear tan points (on the muzzle, above each eye, at the base and rims of the ears, under the tail, on the chest, and on each foot extending partway up each leg), puppies are born black and tan. Yorkies have a gene that causes the black hair to fade to gray with maturity, so only when the adult coat comes in will the color begin to

FYI: Biewer Yorkies

Although spotted (also called piebald or parti-color) Yorkies are not permissible according to the Yorkshire Terrier standard, there's no denying that some people prefer them. In 1984 a Yorkie litter was born in Germany that contained a piebald puppy, which was named Schneeflocken von Friedheck (better known as "Snowflake"). The gene that creates the piebald pattern is recessive, and this puppy's breeders claimed it must have been behind both parents. Because the breeders also raised Shih Tzu, however, some people believe that Snowflake may have had Shih Tzu behind him, accounting for the piebald pattern. Others have pointed out that Maltese and Yorkie crosses can also share this pattern.

Whatever the true story, Snowflake's breeders decided to breed more piebald Yorkies, calling them "Biewer Yorkshire a la Pom Pons," later shortened to Biewer Yorkies. Biewers became popular in Germany, where a club for them was established in 2003. The Biewer is registered and shown in some countries, but not by any major registry in the United States. The American Canine Registry recognizes them and is associated with the Biewer Yorkie Association. Some breeders try to re-create Biewer Yorkies by crossing Yorkies to Shih Tzu or Maltese, but all true Biewer Yorkies trace back to Snowflake's parents, Darling von Friedheck and Fru-Fru von Friedheck.

The Biewer Yorkie standard allows dogs to weigh between 4 and 13 pounds, more than the Yorkshire Terrier standard. It calls for the coat to be colored on no less than 25 percent of its total body area, with black, blue, or chocolate bands. Symmetrical white areas on the face are preferred but not mandatory. For the complete standard, visit the Biewer Yorkie Association at *www.geocities.com/ bieweryorkieassociation.*

gray out. It may take as long as three years for the coat to reach its adult blue color. The tan points of puppies may have black hairs interspersed in them so that they have a sooty appearance; these, too, should clear as the puppy ages so that the tan is a clear, rich color. At 12 weeks of age, expect Yorkie puppies to have black body coats with sooty tan points. Some Yorkies never gray out, and some gray out too much, so the body coat is silver. As puppies, however, it's impossible to predict future coat imperfections.

Small white spots on the chest, head, or feet will usually disappear with maturity, but larger patches will remain. Puppies that are born white with colored patches, all black, all gray, all chocolate, gray and tan, chocolate and tan, or anything else but black and tan will never develop the proper coloration.

Yorkie puppies are born with short hair. At 12 weeks of age it is long enough to look tousled, but it will be several months before it begins to hang. Puppies with thick, heavy coats tend to grow into adults with coats of a wooly or cottony texture, whereas those with thin, silky coats are more likely to grow into adults with the correct silky texture.

Health Testing

Many new owners think "health testing" means that a puppy has received a health certificate from a veterinarian. A veterinary exam can be valuable for giving you a snapshot of the puppy's health when you buy him. A veterinarian should be able to diagnose an open fontanel or hydrocephalus, as well as many communicable diseases, but she won't be able to predict future disorders with a hereditary basis.

When used by responsible dog breeders, "health testing" refers to testing the parents for hereditary disorders. The YTCA recommends the following tests and certifications for breeding stock.

Suggested tests:

- Patellar luxation (see page 91): Orthopedic Foundation for Animals evaluation.
- Eye disorders (see page 89): Canine Eye Registry Foundation evaluation. Prior to the onset of breeding. Evaluations are recommended at 1, 3, and 6 years of age.

Optional tests:

- Legg-Calvé-Perthes (see page 92): Orthopedic Foundation for Animals evaluation.
- Autoimmune thyroiditis: Orthopedic Foundation for Animals evaluation from an approved laboratory. Evaluations are recommended at 1, 3, and 6 years of age.
- Hip dysplasia: Orthopedic Foundation for Animals evaluation.

CHECKLIST

Is the Puppy Healthy?

✔ The skin should not have parasites, hair loss, crusts, or reddened areas.

✔ The eyes, ears, and nose should be free of discharge.

✔ None of the puppies should be coughing, sneezing, or vomiting.

✔ The area around the anus should have no hint of irritation or recent diarrhea.

✔ Puppies should be neither thin nor potbellied.

✔ The gums should be pink, not pale.

✔ The eyelids and lashes should not fold in on the eyes.

✔ By the age of 12 weeks, males should have both testicles descended into the scrotum.

✔ Avoid any puppy that is making significant breathing sounds, including excessive wheezing or snorting.

✔ The breeder should have supplied the puppy's vaccinations and worming records.

✔ You should make any sale contingent on a veterinary exam performed within three days.

DNA tests:

- Progressive retinal atrophy: Although not widespread, a hereditary type of eye disease called progressive rod-cone degeneration, a type of progressive retinal atrophy inherited recessively, can cause blindness in Yorkies. A DNA test can tell if either or both parents carry the recessive gene. If so, they should not be bred to each other. The test is available from *www.optigen.com*.

Yorkies that undergo all of these tests are listed at the Canine Health Information Center (CHIC) Website at *www.caninehealthinfo.org*.

Bile acid test for liver shunt. An important health test that is seldom performed is a bile acid test for porto-systemic (liver) shunt (see page 102). A university study found that liver shunt was 36 times more common in Yorkshire Terriers than in all other breeds combined. The bile acids can be tested at 18 weeks of age. Those that are abnormal seldom become normal after this age. Unfortunately, at 18 weeks, most Yorkies are already in their new homes.

Breed Truths

Open Fontanels

In some very small breeds, including Yorkies, you may feel a soft spot on top of the head where parts of the skull have not yet knitted together. This is called an open fontanel, or molera. If it's small, it will probably close up by a few months of age, but if it's large, it may persist throughout life. Open fontanels are more common in tiny Yorkies. They require extra diligence to prevent the dog from being hit in the molera, which could cause brain damage.

Pedigree

If you only want your Yorkie as a pet, why should you care about his pedigree? First, it's a matter of history and interest that attests to the care and thought behind your puppy's breeding. You can actually trace your Yorkie's lineage back to the first AKC-registered Yorkshire Terriers, although the pedigree you get with your dog will only go back a few generations. Those generations are the ones of most interest, however.

Read a pedigree from left to right, with your puppy's litter on the left, its sire to the right and above, and its dam to the right and below. Avoid inbred pedigrees, in which the same dog appears as an ancestor of both your puppy's sire and dam. The fewer generations between that dog and the litter generally means a more inbred litter. Although inbreeding is a tool used by many breeders, there is little to be gained by the average pet owner in having an inbred dog. Inbreeding increases the chance of two recessive genes appearing in a puppy, heightening the risk of certain health problems.

Look for titles such as CH (Champion) before the name or various obedience and performance titles (see pages 120–123) after the name. Titles can give you an idea not only of the quality of the pedigree, but of how serious the breeder is in producing quality puppies.

Your purebred Yorkshire Terrier should come with the following paperwork:

- AKC registration slip,
- bill of sale,
- copy of the pedigree,

- record of the puppy's medical information,
- any contract or health guarantee,
- contact information in case of future questions, and
- care instructions.

Most AKC puppies are sold as part of a registered litter. The next step is to register each one individually. Unless it's an older dog, the breeder will seldom have done this. Instead you will be given the registration paper to fill in and send to the AKC. Usually you will get to select a name for your puppy. AKC registration is a bargain. It comes with a free 60-day trial health care policy, a free first visit with a participating veterinarian, a puppy care brochure, e-mail certificates for deals at *dog.com*, and of course, a registration certificate. It also enables your dog to participate in AKC events.

You can buy a certified pedigree from the AKC, but you don't really need one. Only on rare occasions, such as if you're trying to register your dog in a foreign country as well, will you need a certified pedigree. The one you receive from your breeder is usually typed or handwritten, and may even claim to be official, but it's not certified.

You can also purchase a DNA profile for your dog. The AKC will send you, upon request, a swab to collect cells from the inner lip of your dog. Send the swab back in a special envelope along with a small fee, and a few months later you'll receive a certificate suitable for framing that shows the pattern of several marker genes that are used in verifying parentage. They won't tell you if your dog has a particular gene-causing disease, but they will identify your dog as well as any fingerprint. Mostly, it's just neat to have.

Breed Truths

Tail Docking

Tail docking is against the law in many countries, but it is customary for Yorkies in America. If you don't plan to show your Yorkie, there's no reason to have a docked tail; even if you do plan to show, Yorkies can compete undocked. If the tail is not docked within the first three days of a puppy's life, it is too late to dock it, except in cases where tail trauma demands it.

Puppy Personality

Yorkie puppies should be friendly toward you, jumping up and clambering into your lap, at least until they get distracted by the next bit of entertainment. Avoid a puppy that:

- hides or runs from you,
- is interested in everything but you to the point of ignoring you,
- growls or snaps at you unless in play, or
- freezes, cringes, or urinates when you pick him up.

PERSONALITY POINTERS
Puppy Aptitude Test

Social attraction Measures sociability and dependence.	The tester coaxes the puppy toward her.
Following Measures dependence versus independence.	The tester walks away.
Restraint Measures dominance versus submissiveness.	The tester gently rolls the puppy on his back and holds him there.
Social dominance Measures dominance versus submissiveness.	The tester strokes the standing puppy on the back.
Elevation dominance Measures acceptance of dominance when the puppy has no control.	The tester lifts the pup slightly off the ground and holds him there.
Retrieving	The tester tosses a crumpled-up piece of paper.
Sound sensitivity	The tester makes a sharp noise a few feet from the puppy.
Touch sensitivity	The tester presses the webbing between the toes.
Sight sensitivity	The tester jerks a towel on a string near the puppy.

Puppy Aptitude Testing

Many breeders and puppy buyers place great confidence in aptitude testing when it comes to choosing puppies. Puppy aptitude tests were developed for choosing the best candidates for guide dogs, and have since been modified for companion dogs.

Puppy aptitude tests can give you a hint of how the puppies in a litter measure up against each other and puppies from other litters. Optimally, they are given as close to 49 days old as possible, and the tester should be a stranger to the puppy. If your heart is set on a puppy but he doesn't fare well on the test, come back and try him again. The tests are far from infallible and, in fact, probably don't have that much predictive value for adult behavior. But they can evaluate the puppy at the time when you take him home. And they're fun! The test consists of nine parts (see chart above).

Does the puppy come eagerly, eventually, or not at all?	The faster the puppy comes, the better.
Does the puppy follow eagerly, hesitantly, or not at all?	The more eagerly the puppy follows, the better.
Does the puppy fight it, eventually relax, or give up immediately?	The more a puppy fights, the greater his tendency to be dominant.
Does the puppy protest, lick the tester, try to escape, or roll over?	An intermediate response is usually best.
Does the puppy struggle fiercely, accept it, try to lick, or freeze?	An intermediate response is usually best.
Does the pup fetch it, grab it and run away, or just look?	A pup that runs after it and brings it back is a better dog for retrieving.
Does the puppy bark at it, look at it, or cringe?	Barking or looking are good responses.
How long does it take the puppy to protest?	A medium sensitivity is probably best.
Does the puppy give chase, just look, or run away?	A puppy that looks is probably best for most pets.

Still can't decide? There's nothing wrong with choosing the puppy that seems to choose you, or with letting the breeder choose the puppy. After all, there's no way you can get to know them in the short time you'll be there like the breeder has gotten to know them.

Chapter Four

Caring for a Yorkie Puppy

The next few months will be some of the most exciting and, at times, frustrating ones of your life with your new Yorkie. They are also the most important ones. The foundations you lay now can make the difference between a good relationship and a bad one, and even life and death. So take the trouble to do it right—and have fun!

Yorkie Shopping List

Yorkies love their people, but let's face it: They love their creature comforts as well. And when it comes to being materialistic, they're at the front of the line! Once your Yorkie recognizes your local pet superstore sign, give up on letting him stay in the car while you shop. But then, half the fun of having a Yorkie is being able to spoil him silly.

Consider the following items for your shopping spree:

Crate. Crates come in three types: wire, which fold flat and have better ventilation; plastic, which are cozy and are approved for airline shipping; and cloth, which are lightweight but can be shredded by dogs who want out. Wait until your Yorkie is good in a crate before trying a cloth one.

Stroller. Dog strollers are essentially soft mesh crates on a stroller platform. You could probably make your own, but the ones sold through pet supply catalogs will be the most stylish way to go. (*Optional.*)

Exercise pen. An exercise pen (X-pen) is a 4-foot by 4-foot pen that you can set up inside. It's safer than locking your puppy in a bathroom, and he's less likely to object because it doesn't have that closed-in feeling that a small room gives him. Choose one that's about 2 feet high. Set the pen in your kitchen or den, where he can be out from underfoot yet still part of the family when you can't watch him. You can also take the X-pen on trips so you have a portable yard—especially handy at rest stops or campgrounds. (*Optional.*)

Baby gates. Baby gates allow your dog more freedom while still blocking off restricted areas. Don't use the old-fashioned accordion style, which

CHECKLIST

Yorkie-Proofing

First on your list is to make your house safe for—and from—your Yorkshire terrorist.

Check all over your house for:

✔ uncovered electrical outlets—can cause shocks

✔ open stairways, decks, or balconies—can cause falls

✔ unsecured doors—can allow escapes, or slam shut on a puppy

Check the kitchen for:

✔ open cabinets holding cleaners and degreasers—can invite poisoning

✔ accessible garbage pails holding enticing rancid food and splintering bones—can invite poisoning, sickness, or gut injury

✔ plastic wraps that can be swallowed—can lodge in intestines

Check the dining room for:

✔ hanging tablecloths that, if pulled, can bring dishes crashing down on the puppy—can crush or otherwise injure a puppy

✔ swinging doors—can trap a puppy's head and neck

Check the family room for:

✔ fireplace without a secure fire screen—can burn a puppy

✔ craft or sewing kits—needles and threads can be swallowed, causing severe injury and illness

✔ heavy statues or vases—can fall on a puppy

Check the bedrooms for:

✔ children's toys—a puppy can chew off pieces

✔ open closets, especially shoe closets—a puppy can chew up your shoes

Check the bathrooms for:

✔ pills and medicines—only takes a few to poison a puppy

✔ hair treatments—can cause eye injuries

✔ drain cleaners—can poison or cause eye injuries

✔ razors—can be swallowed, cutting up mouth and gut

✔ diaper pails—disposable diapers can be eaten and can swell in stomach

Check the garage for:

✔ antifreeze—tastes sweet, but even one swallow can cause fatal kidney failure

✔ fuels, cleaners, paints—can be toxic

✔ batteries—battery acid can be toxic

✔ nails and screws—can be swallowed and cause gut injuries

✔ herbicides, insecticides, and fertilizers—can be toxic

✔ rodent bait—can be enticing to eat, but fatal

Check the yard for:

✔ weak fence—can allow a puppy to escape and be harmed

✔ rotted limbs—can fall on a puppy

✔ unfenced pool—can drown a puppy; always have a way for a dog to climb out, and teach him to find and use it

✔ cocoa mulch—contains theobromine, which is poisonous to dogs

✔ fruit and nut trees—some nuts and fruit parts are poisonous; they can also fall on a puppy's head

✔ pointed sticks at eye level—can poke into a running puppy's eye

✔ predators—can go off with a small dog

✔ treated lawns—can be treated with toxic chemicals that a puppy may lick off his paws

✔ poisonous plants—can be eaten

can close on a puppy's neck. If you don't care about home fashion, just prop a long, sturdy piece of cardboard or wood across your doorway.

Fence. If you have a yard and plan to let your Yorkie loose in it, you need a fence. The Yorkie's terrier heritage makes him a gifted digger and squirmer, so pay special attention to the bottom of the fence and any gaps. The fence also needs to be at least 4 feet tall, preferably even taller, not to prevent your Yorkie from jumping out, but to prevent stray and possibly aggressive dogs from jumping in. (That's the problem with underground electric fences: They can keep your little dog in, but they can't keep other bad dogs out.) Ideally, a fenced area extends from the back door so you can just open the door to let him out.

Kennel. If you plan to leave your Yorkie outside while you can't supervise, invest in a covered kennel run for his protection from the elements and predators. Don't place a run or pen in the back of the yard where your dog will feel lonely and forgotten. (*Optional.*)

Bed. Beds can range from a cardboard box to a miniature bedroom suite to match your own. But leave the fancy ones until your dog is fully grown and over his chewing urges. For now, a cushion or blanket placed inside the crate will do fine.

Anti-chew spray. Like an off-limits sign for your furniture legs, these sprays taste so bitter your puppy will practically foam at the mouth if he tries to chew on something with the spray on it. (*Optional.*)

Collar or harness. Not just a fashion statement, a collar or harness is a means of controlling and identifying your dog. A harness is generally a good idea for Yorkies because it can't damage their trachea like a collar can. A harness lets him pull without stressing his neck or throat. In case of emergency, you could actually lift your dog up by it from the leash, whereas a collar would slip off. But if you do have him wear a collar, make sure it's loose enough for you to get a couple of fingers between it and your puppy's neck, but not so loose that it could slide over his head when walking on leash. Don't leave any collar on a puppy unattended because pups have a talent for getting their lower jaw stuck in it.

Leash. Start with a sturdy, lightweight leash, 4 to 6 feet long. Don't get a chain leash, which are too heavy for a tiny Yorkie.

Retractable leash. These give your dog more freedom, but too many people give them so much freedom that the dog wanders into the road, up to strange dogs, or under people's feet. Retractable leashes should be retracted unless you're in a safe place away from other people and dogs. Be sure to get one made for small dogs; otherwise, they take too much strength to pull for a tiny Yorkie! (*Optional.*)

Identification. Almost any large pet supply store sells identification tags you can make on the spot. Get one.

Coat or sweater. You may not think your Yorkie needs anything but his natural coat, but the Yorkie's coat is long rather than thick. Its lack of undercoat, combined with the Yorkie's small body size, make your little fellow susceptible to chills. Chances are he'll appreciate a coat or sweater in cool weather.

Purse carrier. Part of the fun of having a tiny dog is being able to take him so many places. And as much as he'd rather walk, it's simply not safe for him to do so in crowds, and many public places will only allow dogs in carriers. Shop for one that's well ventilated, sturdy, and gives him a good view.

Cleaning supplies. For rug accidents, use an enzymatic carpet cleaner, which destroys the odor-causing molecules rather than simply covering them up.

Poop scoop. If you have a yard, don't try to clean it with makeshift trowels and buckets; use a tool designed to make the job easy. Two-part scoops are easier to use than hinged versions. Scoops with a rake on one side are better for grass, and the flat-edge pusher varieties are better for cement surfaces.

Poop bags. A variety of special doggy poop disposal bags are available, but you can also use a baby diaper disposal bag or a cheap sandwich bag.

Indoor plumbing. Whether for training purposes or a long-term solution, various indoor potties can make your life much easier. They range from scented pads that entice dogs to use them to sophisticated indoor sod boxes that rinse the grass automatically. (*Optional.*)

Bowls. You can use your own bowls or buy dog bowls. Stainless steel bowls are easy to clean and durable. Ceramic bowls have the disadvantage of chipping. Plastic bowls are the least preferred, because the scratches hold germs, and a few dogs are allergic to them.

Self-feeding and self-watering bowls. These bowls refill when depleted. Just make sure to check that they're still full every day. The disadvantage is that they make it hard to monitor your dog's eating and drinking, and food and water can become old and stagnant. You still have to wash the bowl regularly. (*Optional.*)

Brush. A soft-bristle brush is ideal for getting your puppy used to grooming. Later, you can buy more appropriate grooming tools for his longer coat.

Rinseless shampoo. When you can't give your dog a real bath, just squirt some rinseless shampoo on him, rub it in, and wipe the dirt away with a towel. (*Optional.*)

Grooming table. A table with a grooming arm can save your back and keep your dog under control. (*Optional.*)

Toothbrush. For now, you just need a soft baby toothbrush and some doggy toothpaste, so you can get your puppy used to the feel of having his teeth brushed.

Toenail clippers. You need to start clipping the tips of your puppy's nails now so he can get used to it. Cat nail clippers work fine for most Yorkies, especially puppies.

Plush toys. Puppies love soft, fuzzy toys. Make sure no parts can come off, and that your puppy can't gut it and swallow any noisemakers. Avoid bean or Styrofoam stuffing.

Throw toys. Balls and other toys, such as tug toys, that encourage playing with people are especially good for social development. Studies have shown that dogs that don't get a chance to retrieve as puppies are far less likely to do as adults. Consider cat toys for little Yorkie puppies.

Interactive toys. Toys that challenge your puppy to dislodge food treats can occupy him while you're away. Rotate several interactive toys with different challenges to prevent him from getting bored.

Behavioral Development

Your Yorkie puppy's behavior has already undergone dramatic changes before he's come to live with you, but he has plenty more he needs to accomplish before he's thinking and acting like an adult. Actually, he may act like a puppy for the rest of his life—that's part of the Yorkie allure!

Intellectual Timeline

Birth–seven weeks

- He starts to eat semi-solid food by 3 weeks, and by 5 weeks is eating mostly solid food. The food he eats now will have a long-lasting influence on his adult preferences. If he eats only one food, he'll be cautious of novel foods. If he eats a variety, he'll prefer a variety.
- His dam no longer cleans up his wastes after he starts eating solid food. If he can, he'll totter away from his sleeping spot to do his duty. He's too young to learn housetraining concepts.
- By 7 weeks of age he's starting to be a little more cautious about new places and new things. He knows one person from another, and prefers those he knows.
- As with human babies, early stimulation is vital for development.
- He can learn the concept of clicker training, and some simple commands. The first commands he learns will tend to be his "go-to" commands for the rest of his life; when he wants something, or is confused about what you want, he'll tend to "go to" that behavior. Stick with the standards, like sitting.
- Try some simple leash training. Use a lightweight cat leash. Just put the leash on him and let him lead you around. Then entice him a few feet in the direction you want to go by dangling a treat just in front of him. Give it to him when he walks there.

Breed Needs

Age at Placement

Because of their small size, Yorkies should optimally not be placed in their new homes until they are 12 weeks of age, later than what is suggested for most breeds. However, in recognition that many, if not most, Yorkies are placed before this optimal age, the directions in this book attempt to encompass both situations, earlier and later.

Eight–twelve weeks
- Bonding with his canine family has reached its highest point at 7 weeks of age. It will gradually decline until he's 10 weeks old, after which he will prefer his human family.
- His play is getting rougher and he's using his mouth on everything. Handing him a toy often distracts him from chewing on you, but if not, do what his littermates would do when he plays too rough: say "ouch," and refuse to play until he calms down.
- He is eager to learn, and works well for either food or play.
- Now is the time to enroll him in puppy kindergarten class.

Three–six months
- He still objects to being separated from his family, whether canine or human. Keep giving him short periods alone. Studies have shown that soft stuffed toys, warm toys with a heartbeat, or toys with a safe mirror can help alleviate his distress somewhat.
- At no other time in your puppy's life is he more amenable to training, but by about 4 months of age the ease with which puppies learn actually starts to decline. Be sure you've introduced him to the concept of learning before then.

- He can easily learn how to sit, lie down, stay, come, and heel by 4 months of age. If you have aspirations to compete in advanced obedience, or in agility, hunting, or trailing, now's the time to introduce him to the concepts of climbing over and under objects, and of using his nose to seek out hidden objects.
- Now is the time to enroll in an elementary puppy training class.

Seven–twelve months
- He's still finding his place in the pack. Older dogs are now less tolerant of his transgressions. Keep an eye on them, but remember that the adult needs to lay down the rules to the youngster, and better now than later.
- He may try to push your limits, ignore your commands, and see what he can get away with. Deal with disobedience firmly, steering him toward more rewarding behaviors.
- Males that have not been castrated may start lifting their legs when they are 8 to 12 months of age, and some do it inside the house. This is a hard habit to break and one you absolutely must try to nip in the bud by watching him carefully and rushing him outside with a disapproving tone if you catch him in the act. A female may start to urinate more often as she comes into estrus and, especially, during estrus.
- He's reasoning more like an adult. Certain tests of memory and reasoning, such as "object permanence" (a test in which the dog detects that an object that was once there has been removed when he wasn't looking), show that dogs don't develop that ability until 8 or 9 months of age.
- He really should know the basics—*sit, down, come, stay, heel*—by now. If you haven't yet enrolled in a class, it's time you did, so he can practice around others. If he is getting bored with the basics, add some tricks or some of the advanced exercises. It's easier for him to learn them now, while he's still in the learning mode.
- If you have special plans for your dog, such as therapy work or search and rescue, it's time to get with a group that can help you train him.

First Impressions

As you introduce your new Yorkie to your home, be selfish. Now is not the time for all the neighbors to visit. It's your time to bond with your new dog. He's confused enough trying to figure out what happened to his old family—and who his new family will be. Introduce him only to these people for now; there will be plenty of time for him to play social butterfly later.

Give him a chance to relieve himself in the area you've decided will be his outdoor bathroom area. It's never too soon to start good habits. Then let him explore in the yard or house, always supervised, of course. He should not have eaten before leaving the breeder's, so fix him a meal and let him eat it in a secure place such as his crate or X-pen. Or maybe your lap! Then take him outside to eliminate again. When he starts to tire, put him in his sleeping quarters.

His first night away from his old family is going to be confusing and, very likely, frightening. Don't even think of making him sleep all by himself in another room. Even if you don't intend for him to stay in your bedroom in the future, make an exception so he has some company at first. Besides, you know you really want him sleeping there!

But he's too little to sleep in your bed, at least not without the protection of a crate. He could wake up and fall off in the night, or you could roll over on him. A crate is the ideal place. The crate should have plenty of soft bedding in it, as well as a stuffed toy he can use as a surrogate littermate. It can be placed on your bed or next to it.

If your puppy is too uneasy to fall asleep all alone, let him fall asleep next to you outside the crate. When he's snoozing soundly, pick him up and place him in the crate. He may awaken momentarily but will fall back asleep. Chances are, he will wake up crying several times the first few nights. Traditional dog-rearing advice warns owners not to give in to the dog's crying. But ignoring him when he most needs reassurance only teaches him that he can't depend on you for help. Some dog behaviorists now believe such a situation may actually contribute to separation anxiety in adulthood. They instead recommend comforting the puppy if he cries so he learns he has some control over his environment. That doesn't mean you spend the rest of your life rushing in at the slightest cry, but it does mean you acknowledge his distress and attend to his basic needs, such as comforting him or taking him to relieve himself. Then you put him back in his bed.

Crate Training

Every dog should be crate trained. Crates give your dog a secure bed of his own and give you a place to put him where you won't worry about him. Crates help in housetraining, provide a safe means of car travel, and serve as a safe haven when staying with friends or at hotels. A crate-trained dog will fare better if he has to be crated at the veterinary office. That doesn't mean your dog should spend hours and hours crated. Think of a crate as your child's crib. It's a safe place to sleep, but not a place to grow up. And it's certainly not a place for punishment.

The crate is one of the safest spots your puppy can be, but you must do your part. Do not leave collars on your puppy while he's in the crate. Collars, especially choke collars or collars with tags, can get caught in crate wires. Soft bedding is wonderful for most puppies, but those that chew and swallow it may have to be relegated to surfaces less likely to cause intestinal blockages. If your puppy tends to chew on the wire, he could get his jaw or tooth caught. Discourage such behavior by spraying the wire with anti-chew preparations and by making sure your pup has no issues with being crated.

Establish a good association with the crate by feeding your dog in it. If he's uneasy about it, just place the food slightly inside the crate at first so he doesn't even have to go inside to eat. Then move it further inside. Finally, close the door while he eats, opening it as soon as he finishes. You can probably do this within the period of a day. Soon he will be running to the crate as soon as he sees you with food. If you want, you can now introduce a cue, such as "Bedtime!," for him to go in the crate.

You can extend his time in the crate by giving him chew toys or interactive toys to occupy him while inside. Extend his time gradually, always trying to let him out before he has a chance to get bored or vocal. If he does begin to protest, wait until he is momentarily quiet before letting him out. Continue to extend the time he must be quiet before he gets released.

Being Alone

It's so much fun to spend time with your new puppy that you may neglect to teach him to be alone once in awhile. Being alone is very stressful to puppies, and even many adults. Your puppy instinctively becomes anxious if he finds himself separated from his caregiver. A puppy that finds himself all alone will cry, howl, and yip, bringing his mother or father on the run. If nobody shows up, he will keep crying until he is too exhausted to continue. Naïve owners may think he has gotten over his angst, but exhaustion is not the same as being OK.

Contrary to popular opinion, crates don't seem to make young pups feel more secure. In fact, crated pups (especially those not already familiar with the crate) tend to cry even more than uncrated pups when separated. That's why it may be better to leave your pup in an exercise pen or small, safe room when you first start teaching him to be home alone. You can leave a crate with an open door accessible to him in case he does prefer it.

Giving your pup something to occupy him and comfort him while you are gone is useful, but it depends on what you give. Studies have shown that mirrors and soft, cuddly toys are most effective at calming separated puppies, but food has little value—probably because distressed puppies are not hungry puppies. Puppies are comforted by soft, warm, dog-shaped toys, some of which even have a heartbeat, simulating the pup's littermates or dam.

Helpful Hints

Exercise Pens

Like all proper terriers, Yorkies were born to explore, and as soon as they can they're poking, sniffing, and chewing on everything in reach. Even if your home is puppy-proofed, you can't let him wander about it unsupervised. Yet you can't keep him crated all the time, either. One solution is to set up one or more exercise pens, or even baby playpens, in your favorite rooms. You can interact with your puppy as you go about your business, letting him out when you won't be distracted by other things.

Housetraining

The best time to start teaching a puppy where to eliminate is between 7 and 9 weeks of age. Before that time, puppies do not seem to learn the concept or control themselves sufficiently. After 9 weeks of age, they seem to prefer using whatever surface or place they were using between 7 and 9 weeks of age. So it is very important that you make sure your pup has as few chances to go in the wrong places, and as many chances to go in the right places, as possible during this crucial time.

This is one reason that toy dogs in general, and especially those bought from pet stores, may be more difficult to housetrain. It's easy to raise toy dogs indoors, and very often such dogs have never had the experience of eliminating outside by the time you bring them home. They don't recognize grass or the great outdoors as a bathroom area, and they are slow to accept it as such.

It doesn't help that the typical dog owner pushes the puppy out the door and leaves him all alone outside, where the puppy protests, cries, and does just about everything but relieve himself. Once let back inside, though, he relaxes enough to wet all over the floor. No matter how busy you are, early housetraining must be a team sport. Go outside with him! And just as you would train any other behavior, lavish him with praise and, more important, treats for eliminating in the right place. Keep a jar of treats by the door and grab a handful when you go outside with him. Wait until he's just finishing, then heap on the praise and give him a treat. Don't wait until you're back inside; that's too late.

A regular schedule is important for housetraining. You can help your puppy to have a regular bowel movement by feeding him on schedule and making sure you don't give him novel foods that may cause diarrhea. You should also take him outside when he awakens, after he eats, and before he goes to bed. You will also need to take him out in between those times. A standard rule of thumb is that a puppy can hold himself for as many hours as he is months old. He can go longer overnight, if you don't let him eat or guzzle down water before bed. That in turn means not encouraging vigorous play, which will make him thirsty, before bedtime. And of course, there are limits. Beyond the age of 8 months, the rule comes to a standstill; no dog should be asked to hold it beyond 8 hours.

Gotta go!

Be responsive to your dog's cues and schedules.

- Immediately after a puppy awakens, he must urinate.
- Within 15 minutes after eating, he must defecate. (The act of eating puts into motion all sorts of peristaltic gut motility.)
- In the middle of playing, he must urinate—a lot.
- If he exercises a lot he'll drink a lot more water, and a while later he'll also have to urinate.
- If he starts whining for no reason, he has a reason, and it's going to smell bad unless you get him outside.
- When you see him sniffing and circling, he's going to go. Get him outside as fast as possible, even if you must carry him there.
- When in doubt, take him out!

Young puppies avoid eliminating in their sleeping and eating areas, so if you restrict your puppy to a small area he's less likely to eliminate there and will make an effort to hold himself until you let him out. You can use the crate as his small area, making sure it's not so large that he can simply use one half of it for his bathroom. If your crate is too large, block off part of it with a box or divider.

Confine your pup when you can't supervise him, but let him out regularly. If you force him to have accidents in his crate, he'll give up trying to hold it at all.

When you let him out, take him immediately to his elimination area. Once he's relieved himself, socialize, play, snuggle, and do all the fun things that make having a puppy worth all the work.

Once he's housetrained using the crate, expand his den area by placing his bed or crate in a tiny enclosed area—an area only a couple of feet beyond the boundary of his bed. Do everything you can to prevent him from soiling this area; that is, keep him on a frequent outdoor bathroom break schedule. Gradually expand his area as he goes without soiling it, until eventually he has access to an entire room, or more.

Housetraining Timeline

Birth–seven weeks
- He needs to explore while he's still fearless. Good experiences at this age will stay with him throughout life, helping him take new situations in stride later on.
- It's a good idea for him to practice sleeping by himself for short stretches. A little crate or bed is perfect for learning to sleep alone, or with a cuddly, warm toy.

Eight–twelve weeks
- After 9 weeks of age, puppies seem to cling to whatever substrate they learned to use for relieving themselves between 7 and 9 weeks of age. Make sure that during this crucial time he's using whatever you want him to use for the rest of his life.
- Expose him to being alone for short periods. If you wait until he's 12 weeks, studies have shown he will have a much more difficult time adjusting. Exposure should be for very short time periods, before he has a chance to become stressed.

Three–six months
- He's only now entering his heavy chewing stage. His baby teeth were capable of decorating everything with tiny pinprick holes, but his adult teeth can do a lot more damage.
- It's not unusual for him to regress when it comes to elimination habits. A good rule of thumb is to not expect him to hold himself for more hours than he is months old. That means your 3-month-old can only hold himself for 3 hours or less, if he's been playing or drinking a lot.

Seven–twelve months
- He's going to need somewhat more exercise than before. He needs to walk around the block, sniff all the neat smells, and see something new every day.

- If he regresses in his housetraining, you need to take a step back in your training. He may look like an adult, but remember: He's been on this earth less than a year.

Dealing with Accidents

All puppies have accidents, and Yorkie puppies seem to have more than their share. If you catch him in the act, give a startling "No!" or "Aght!" and scoop him up to scuttle him outside as quickly as possible. Once outside, be sure to reward him when he goes in the right place.

Unless you catch him in the act, punishment doesn't work, and even then, overzealous punishment only teaches him to be afraid of you. Rubbing your dog's nose in a mess, no matter how recently it was deposited, doesn't do anything but convince him you're strange. Punishing him after the act is counterproductive because your dog seldom knows why you're on a rant and it causes him to distrust you. Also, your unpredictable nature makes him nervous, increasing the likelihood he will have to urinate or defecate.

It's vitally important that you clean up any accidents, not just because you want to still have company come over, but because odors play an important role in signaling puppies and dogs to urinate or defecate. If it's urine, sop up as much as you can. Then drench it in an odor neutralizer. Odor neutralizers, which are available from pet stores, attack the molecules that create the odors. They won't totally destroy them, but you can then have a hope of masking them with a strong scented freshener. The neutralizers only work as long as they are moist, so you can place plastic wrap over the area to keep it

HOME BASICS
Indoor Systems Compared

Dog Litter

Pros
- Highly absorbent material.
- Relatively inexpensive.

Cons
- Dogs can scratch their feet enthusiastically after using it, and may kick litter out of the box.
- Some dogs may play in it

Grid Systems

Pros
- Dog's feet are kept dry.
- Inexpensive.

Cons
- Some dogs may be hesitant to walk or relieve themselves on the grid.
- Plain paper may not attract dogs nor absorb odors adequately.

Sod systems

Pros
- Easy transition for dogs used to going outdoors.
- The ultimate in fashion.
- Fairly expensive.

Cons
- Natural grass must be watered and periodically replaced.
- Dogs may dig.
- Unless rinsed often or sprayed with deodorant, odors may build up.
- Fairly large compared to other systems.

Disposable Pads

Pros
- Easy to manage.
- Great for travel.
- Relatively inexpensive, especially if not used exclusively.

Cons
- Some dogs may rip them up.
- Pads may slide unless held in place.

Washable Pads

Pros
- Reusable.
- Easy to manage.
- Inexpensive in the long run.

Cons
- Not scented with attractants.

moist a little longer. It's impossible to cover the scent with carpet fresheners; dogs have too good a sense of smell for that. Solids are usually easier to pick up, but you should still spray the area afterward. Diarrhea can be a challenge, but even though it may have you considering tile floors, you can do it.

Indoor Plumbing

Many Yorkie owners find that it's convenient to train their dogs to use an indoor potty in addition to going outside. Ranging from simple absorbent pads to self-watering indoor lawns, indoor potties are all the rage for sophisticated Yorkies.

Paper training. Newspaper has been the standard indoor system for generations of puppies and even adults. But wet newspaper stinks, falls apart, and tends to stay wet. Dogs can track urine and even newsprint on their wet feet. Other systems really are better.

Litter boxes. Dogs can be trained to use litter boxes, but you don't want to use cat litter in them. Cat litter is designed to make it easy and enticing for cats to dig—just what you don't want for your dog! It also has a greater tendency to stick to paws and especially to long hair. Finally, dogs are more likely to eat litter, and eating the clumping type of cat litter can be very unhealthy.

Dog litter consists of much larger pellets (about as wide as a pencil and an inch or two in length) made of a mixture of absorbent paper and wood pulp. The pellets allow liquids to drain to the bottom of the pan, and then absorb them from the bottom up, leaving the top layer dry. The litter is placed in a high-sided litter box to accommodate male leg-lifters and dogs that kick after they relieve themselves.

Grid systems. Grid systems consist of a grating that stands above a paper-lined tray, preventing the dog from stepping in urine or the wet papers just below. The paper is changed as needed.

Disposable pads. Another solution to keep your dog's feet dry is to increase absorbency and cover it with a layer of paper that stays dry. Enter the absorbent pads, based on the same concept as highly absorbent baby diapers. At one time such pads were just considered a replacement for newspaper as a housetraining aid, but as more people found they were handy for everyday use, even with adults, the pads' popularity grew. The best pads have a non-slip waterproof backing, absorbent layers, and leak-proof edges, and are scented so that dogs are attracted to them.

Washable pads. One problem with paper pads is that some dogs, especially puppies, like to turn them into confetti. In addition, because they're disposable, using them exclusively over a period of years can get costly and isn't exactly eco-conscious. Many people look at their expense and opt to just put down a scatter rug for the dog to use. The problem is that dogs then generalize to using all scatter rugs in the house, pretty much defeating the purpose. In addition, scatter rugs can be unwieldy to wash. Other owners just use towels, but towels aren't that absorbent and they don't prevent liquids from seeping through to the floor beneath. Besides, who wants to dry off with one after it's been used for that? More savvy owners buy plastic-lined bed pads made for incontinent people. They trap moisture and don't allow it to seep out. Now specially made absorbent bed pads are available for dogs. Many breeders of long-coated toy dogs opt to line their kennel run floors with the pads as they help prevent coat damage that otherwise occurs from urine seeping into the hair.

Sod systems. Sod systems use either real or artificial grass to provide your dog with a miniature indoor yard. You might think you could hammer together some boards, throw in some dirt, and plant some grass, but after a few weeks, you'd see—or at least smell—the problem with that. In order to thwart odors, you need a waterproof frame (not wood), a way to rinse or drain urine, and an easy means to replace sod periodically. These systems can be kept outside on a balcony or inside (in which case you need to change the grass more often). Otherwise you should replace the grass every couple of months, and in between times spray it twice a week with a urine neutralizer to eliminate odors.

Teaching Your Dog to Use an Indoor Potty

If your dog has never been trained to eliminate outside, training him to use an indoor potty is very simple. You use the same vigilance that you would if you were training him to go outside to relieve himself, except that when he appears ready to go, you hustle him to the indoor area. If the system you're using is pre-scented with odors to attract the dog, he may naturally go there. If the system isn't pre-scented, you can capture some urine from your dog and sprinkle it on the area. Dogs tend to relieve themselves where they smell they've gone before.

An indoor pen is a handy training tool. Place the pen on a tile or nonabsorbent floor, or place a plastic liner, such as an old shower curtain, under it. Put the dog's bed and bowls in one corner, leave a space of a few feet, and cover most of the rest of the floor with your potty system of choice. He won't want to use his bed, so by default he will use the potty. That's why you don't want much bare floor in there, especially at first. If you're using a grid system, take the grid part off at first so he gets used to using the papers beneath. As the dog grows more proficient at hitting the target, you can either expand the pen or, if you're using pads, decrease their area, always keeping it as far away from the bed and bowls as possible. Remember to praise and even give your dog a treat for doing this special "trick."

If your dog is already trained to eliminate outside, you may have to start by bringing in actual sod from his outdoor potty area and placing it on the indoor potty. Place the sod on the indoor system, and gradually decrease the amount of area the sod covers. If you're planning to use artificial grass, and your dog is used to real grass, start with real grass and switch once he's used to going inside.

Despite their convenience, indoor potties are no substitute for taking your dog for a walk. An outdoor excursion is meant as more than an elimination break. It gives your dog exercise, social interaction, mental stimulation, and something to look forward to every day. It does the same for you. But there's no reason you can't have both!

Setting Limits

Decide now what areas of your home will be off limits, and use barriers to keep your Yorkie out. Most people allow their Yorkies on the furniture, but if that's not in your plans don't lift him up there. In fact, it's a good idea to sit on the floor with your puppy when you can, since young puppies are apt to launch themselves from the sofa and hurt themselves upon landing. If you do want your puppy on the furniture, make sure he can get down by way of some pillows or other stairway or ramp.

If you want him off the furniture, spend time on the floor with him. Provide him with a bed that's just as soft, maybe in a place with a good view. And if he does get on the furniture, simply lift him down and say "No." Teach him to go to his bed on cue by rewarding him when he goes there on his own. As he starts to eagerly run to his bed, give him the cue "Place!" and reward him once he's there.

Stop the Chewing!

Even the best-behaved puppies chew, not only when they are teething, but at least until they're a year old. When you find your puppy chewing on your belongings, take the object from him and replace it with a more acceptable object. Make sure the object you give him in exchange does not resemble anything of yours you don't want him to chew. That means no old shoes! No socks, no stuffed animals (if you have children who collect them), nothing that resembles anything he can find around the house. What your puppy learns to chew on at an early age will tend to be what he looks for to chew on for the rest of his life.

Assemble a group of dog toys and only let your puppy have a few at a time, rotating them every few days so he has the excitement of new toys. Be sure to include some interactive toys, such as those he must work at in order to extract food. You can fill these with bones, soft cheese, canned dog food, or peanut butter, and then freeze them to make them last even longer. Some toys dispense kibble a piece at a time as the toy is rolled. Some toys are meant to be soaked in water and frozen, providing your puppy a cold teething toy. With luck, your Yorkie will prefer these fancy toys to your fancy belongings.

Socialization

Puppies start off life relatively fearless, but at about 5 weeks of age, they gradually start to get more cautious of new situations and people. Sometime after 12 weeks of age the fear response becomes the dominant one, making it difficult for the puppy to accept situations he has never before experienced. This means that you have a deadline to meet, a deadline before which you need to make sure your puppy has experienced a wide range of people, places, and things to prepare him for the rest of his life.

It's the quality, not quantity, that counts when socializing. Good intentions can too often lead to bad results if you overwhelm your pup. As with all things puppy, you need to introduce new experiences gradually, never pushing your puppy past the point that he's scared. Fear is easy to learn but hard to unlearn.

Your aim is to have your puppy comfortable around strange people, dogs, animals, places, and situations. Introduce him to different floorings, stairs, car rides, and things he'll be doing later in life.

Remember, you want introductions to go well, so it's a good idea if you have control over how meetings go. Ask friends to come over and to greet

the puppy as strangers should, which means kneeling down and rubbing him under the chin or on the chest. You'll want your puppy to meet men, women, people in wheelchairs, people with canes, and people of all races, ages, and sizes.

Don't take your puppy to a crowd with the idea of letting him meet lots of people at once. He could be stepped on, or people could start trying to reach for him to pet him all at once, and he could end up being terrified. It's better for your puppy to meet a few well-chosen people under good circumstances than a horde of humans under overwhelming circumstances.

By 12 weeks of age, your dog should have had at least three good experiences with each of the following:

✔ 10 different people of different races, sex, and age, including children
✔ Person in wheelchair, and with walker or cane.
✔ People wearing sunglasses, hats, and raincoats.
✔ 5 different dogs of different sizes
✔ Riding in cars
✔ Being crated
✔ Being alone
✔ Walking on slick surfaces
✔ Walking up and down three steps
✔ Retrieving
✔ Any special abilities for future work

And just because he passes the 12-week milestone, don't quit. He needs refresher exposures over the next months as well.

Socialization Timeline

Birth–seven weeks
• For the first 3 weeks he prefers his dam to anyone.
• By 4 weeks he prefers his littermates. Playing with them teaches him to relate to other dogs, and may be important for learning to inhibit his bites.
• Once people begin to feed him, he begins to attend more to them.
• By 7 weeks, he actively prefers people to his dam.

Eight–twelve weeks
• Starting at around 7 or 8 weeks, puppies gradually become more fearful of novel situations, until, by 12 weeks, they are more distrustful than trustful. That means you need to expose your puppy to as many situations as he'll encounter later in life as you can before this deadline.

Three–six months
• By 12 weeks of age, his tendency to be cautious of new things has overwhelmed his tendency to be curious about them, and that tendency will increase for the next few months. That doesn't mean he should be sheltered. You need to continue exposing him to new people, places, and things, taking extra care to make sure he has good experiences. You may have to take things more slowly than you could have at a younger age.
• Social positions with any littermates gradually become more stable, until the ranking order is fairly constant by week 16.

Seven–twelve months
• He's getting surer of himself, maybe even cocky. But at around 8 to 9 months he undergoes a second fearful stage, when little negative experiences make a big impact on him. So continue to get him out and about, but with a watchful eye.

Play

Don't forget the play! Yorkie puppies love to play, and it's important for them to play with you, even if your dog has other pets to play with. Put the other pets away and devote several periods a day to various types of play. Roll balls, wave feathers, drag cat toys, and play tug. Hide treats and let him find them. Play is important both intellectually and socially. And it's one of the reasons people have dogs! Even after your Yorkie grows up, playing with him will keep him young at heart—and you, too.

Play Development Timeline

Birth–seven weeks
- Be sure to introduce balls and other toys to him, since puppies also learn specific play habits at an early age.

Eight–twelve weeks
- Now is the time to introduce him to the concept of fetch. Puppies not exposed to the idea of fetch at that early age have difficulty understanding it later.

Three–six months
- His games still center around play fighting, but you need to redirect his games to something more cooperative. Try some fetch; if he won't bring

the ball back, practice in a hallway. Use two balls, stand midway down the hall, and throw one ball to one end. Once he gets it, encourage him to come back—use a treat if you have to—and when he gets to you, throw the other ball in the other direction. Keep it up until he knows his reward for bringing you one ball is the chance to chase another.

- He's ready for some more sophisticated toys. Various puzzle and inter- active toys require him to work to get treats or toys out of them. Such toys are great for occupying his mind when you can't be with him.

Seven–twelve months

- Try new, more complicated toys. Rotate his toys, so it seems to him he's getting new ones every few days.
- A lot of his play now centers on showing you how much faster, stronger and smarter he is than you. You can play along, but make sure you win, or that you are the one to say when the game is over.

Physical Development

The first few months of your Yorkie's life is a time not only of astounding behavioral changes, but physical ones as well. One of the most common questions of new owners is that of how large their puppy will grow.

The average weight of a Yorkshire Terrier at birth is between 2.5 ounces (about 71 grams) and 5.5 ounces (about 155 grams). Puppies may lose a little weight the first day, but after that should steadily gain, almost dou- bling their weight by 1 week of age.

Between 2 and 16 weeks of age, a Yorkie puppy that was 2.5 ounces at birth will gain about an ounce a week, whereas one that was about 5.5 ounces at birth will gain about 3 ounces a week.

It's difficult to predict adult weight, but one often-used formula is to take the height and weight at age 12 weeks and double them. The adult weight should be within about 5 ounces, or 255 grams, plus or minus.

Use the chart on the next page for a rough idea of adult weight. To use it,

Helpful Hints

Helping Ears Stand

By 6 to 8 weeks of age, most Yorkie puppy ears are standing upright, but a few, especially larger ears, may need a little help. You can train the ears to stand like this:

1. Carefully shave the top half of the ears, front and back.
2. Using masking tape, tape each ear so it folds forward in on itself vertically, coming to a point at the top. Do not make it too tight! You don't want to cut off circulation.
3. You may also wish to tape the two ears together with another piece of tape so that they stand upright.
4. Remove the tape every three days or sooner, if it gets wet— never leave wet tape on the ear! If the ear is standing, leave it alone. If it isn't, tape for another three days.

Weight Chart

Age	Weight in ounces (grams)							
Birth	2.5 (70)	3.0 (85)	3.5 (99)	4.0 (113)	4.5 (128)	5.0 (142)	5.5 (155)	6.0 (170)
1 week	4.5 (128)	5.5 (155)	6.0 (170)	7.0 (198)	8.0 (227)	9.0 (255)	9.5 (269)	10.0 (284)
2 weeks	6 (170)	7 (198)	8.5 (241)	10 (284)	12 (340)	13 (369)	13.5 (383)	14 (397)
3 weeks	7 (198)	8.5 (241)	10 (284)	13 (369)	15 (425)	16 (454)	17 (482)	18 (510)
4 weeks	8 (227)	10 (284)	12 (340)	15 (425)	18 (510)	20 (567)	21 (595)	22 (624)
6 weeks	10 (284)	13 (369)	15 (425)	17 (482)	22 (624)	24 (680)	27 (765)	30 (850)
8 weeks	12 (340)	16 (454)	19 (539)	22 (624)	26 (737)	29 (822)	32 (907)	35 (992)
10 weeks	14 (397)	20 (567)	24 (680)	26 (737)	34 (964)	37 (1049)	39 (1106)	42 (1191)
12 weeks	16 (454)	22 (624)	27 (765)	31 (879)	39 (1049)	43 (1219)	46 (1304)	48 (1361)
16 weeks	20 (567)	29 (822)	36 (1021)	39 (1049)	48 (1361)	54 (1531)	60 (1701)	66 (1871)
12 months	32 (907) 2 lb	48 (1361) 3 lb	56 (1588) 3.5 lb	64 (1814) 4 lb	80 (2268) 5 lb	88 (2495) 5.5 lb	96 (2722) 6 lb	104 (2948) 6.5 lb

find the age and weight of your puppy and then follow the column down to the adult age in the last row.

Physical Development Timeline

Birth–seven weeks
- His sense of smell and taste are developed, but his eyes and ears are closed until almost 2 weeks of age.
- He's able to sense warmth right from the start. He can also sense pain. Tail docking, if performed, is usually done within the first three days of birth.
- Teeth begin to emerge at 3 weeks of age, starting with canines.
- The ears are usually standing upright by about 6 to 8 weeks of age.

Eight–twelve weeks

- His vision and hearing are almost adult-like, but not quite. They won't be fully mature until he's 10 weeks old.
- All 28 of his baby teeth are in.
- If he's a boy, both his testicles should be in his scrotum by now. If they're not, and he's destined for the show ring, it's time to consult with your veterinarian.

Three–six months

- Around 4 to 5 months his baby teeth start to be replaced by adult teeth. His incisors will fall out and be replaced by permanent teeth first, followed by his canine teeth and finally his rear teeth. Sometimes the baby canine teeth don't fall out and the new ones comes in beside them. If they stay there for more than a few days or a week it could mess up his occlusion, so you should consult your veterinarian.
- If his ears are not standing upright by 6 months, they probably won't ever stand.
- If you plan to neuter or spay your dog, the best time is at about 5 months of age, giving the dog time to mature but avoiding the chance of doing it after sexual maturity. Spaying before the first estrus greatly reduces the chance of breast cancer in later life.

Seven–twelve months

- He's reached his adult size by now, although he still has some filling out to do.
- All 42 adult teeth should be in by 7 months, and any baby teeth remaining should be examined by a veterinarian. Always X-ray before pulling baby teeth, because not all dogs have permanent ones waiting to erupt in their place.
- Testicles should be permanently in place. If his testicles still haven't descended, it's time to talk to your veterinarian about what to do. At this age, the chance of them coming down is remote. It's not that they're not there; they're retained within his body, where the higher temperature renders them both incapable of creating viable sperm and more likely to become cancerous later in life. For this reason he'll probably need surgery to remove them.
- If not neutered or spayed, your Yorkie is becoming sexually mature. If male, his testicles are growing in size, and his penis, too, and he's showing interest in females in heat. He can probably sire puppies by 9 months of age. Females usually have their first estrus season between 6 and 10 months of age.

Teeth

Yorkie puppies start to shed their baby teeth between 4 and 7 months of age. Sometimes a permanent tooth will come in before the baby tooth has fallen out, growing in alongside it. This is especially common with the canine teeth (fangs). If this condition persists for more than about four days, ask your veterinarian if the baby tooth should be pulled. If it stays in too long, it could cause overcrowding (already a problem in Yorkie mouths) and misalignment of teeth. If it's not causing too much of a problem, your veterinarian may advise you to wait and either hope it falls out on its own or have it removed when you have your dog spayed or neutered.

Feeding

Feed your Yorkie puppy a good-quality puppy food. For more information on nutrition in general, see Chapter Six. The major thing to know about Yorkie puppies is that they must eat often. Young Yorkie puppies are prone to a dangerous condition called hypoglycemia, which is caused by low blood sugar. Very young or small dogs cannot store enough glucose as glycogen, and when these dogs don't eat often enough, or if they use a lot of energy from playing or being stressed, the body depletes its stores of glycogen and has to start breaking down body fat for energy. But because small puppies don't have much body fat, that energy doesn't last long, and the body runs out of sufficient energy. The brain depends on this energy and is one of the first systems to fail. The puppy becomes abnormally sleepy, weak,

and uncoordinated, and may not even eat when offered food. If he doesn't eat, the condition can progress to the point that the puppy has seizures, loses consciousness, and dies.

This is why young Yorkie puppies, especially small ones, must eat frequently, at least every four hours during the daytime. At night, when you can't feed them as often, they must be kept warm and quiet so they don't expend a lot of energy. Meals should be fairly high in protein, fat, and complex carbohydrates. Avoid foods with simple sugars, such as sweets and

BE PREPARED! In Case of Hypoglycemia

If you suspect your puppy is having a hypoglycemic episode:

1. Feed him a food high in simple sugar, such as corn syrup. If he can't eat, rub it on his gums but don't try to force it down his throat.
2. Keep him warm.
3. Call the veterinarian. You may need to go there for intravenous glucose.
4. If the corn syrup works, he should be better within minutes. If he is, feed him a small, high-protein meal such as meat baby food.
5. If the corn syrup does not work, try again and rush him to the veterinarian.

semi-moist foods. The exception is if your puppy is already showing signs of hypoglycemia.

A young Yorkie puppy should be fed four to five times a day. Let him eat as much as he wants. From about 4 to 7 months of age, you can feed him four times a day. From 7 to 9 months of age, feed him three times a day, and then gradually cut down to twice a day by the time he's 12 months old.

Most Yorkies outgrow hypoglycemia by the time they are 7 months of age. Until then, feed frequent meals, have corn syrup in your pantry, and be aware of the warning signs.

Puppy Health

Vaccinations

Without well-timed vaccinations, your Yorkie can be vulnerable to deadly communicable diseases. Your pup received his early immunity through his dam's colostrum during the first few days of nursing. As long as he still has that immunity, any vaccinations you give him won't provide additional immunity. But after several weeks that immunity begins to decrease. As his immunity falls, both the chance of a vaccination being effective and the chance of getting a communicable disease rise. The problem is that immunity diminishes at different times in different dogs. So starting at around 6 weeks of age, a series of vaccinations is given in order to catch the time when they will be effective while leaving as little unprotected time as possible. During this time of uncertainty it's best not to take your puppy to places where unvaccinated dogs may congregate. Some deadly viruses, such as parvovirus, can remain in the soil for six months after an infected dog has shed the virus in its feces there.

Vaccinations are divided into core vaccines, which are advisable for all dogs, and noncore vaccines, which are advisable only for some dogs. Core vaccines are those for rabies, distemper, parvovirus, and hepatitis (using the CAV-2 vaccine, not the CAV-1, which can cause adverse reactions but is still sold by some feed stores). Noncore vaccines include those for leptospirosis, coronavirus, tracheobronchitis, and Lyme disease. Your veterinarian can advise you if your dog's lifestyle and environment put him at risk for these diseases. Remember, more is not necessarily better!

A sample core vaccination protocol for puppies suggests giving a three-injection series at least three weeks apart, with each injection containing distemper, parvovirus, adenovirus 2 (CAV-2), and parainfluenza (CPIV). The series should not end before 16 weeks of age. A booster is given one year later, and then boosters are given every three years. Rabies should be given at 16 weeks of age, with boosters at one- to three-year intervals according to local law.

Leptospirosis vaccine is the vaccination most likely to cause adverse reactions, especially in very young or very small dogs, and for that reason many

FYI: The Heartworm Cycle

- Mosquito feeds on infected dogs, ingesting pre-larval heartworms called microfilaria. (The American Heartworm Society estimates that about 27 million dogs are not protected from heartworms. Heartworm cases are found in all 50 states, but are most prevalent within 150 miles of the Gulf and Atlantic coasts as far north as New Jersey, and along the Mississippi River region. In these areas almost half the dogs not on heartworm prevention are infected.)
- Microfilaria mature into larvae and move to mosquito's mouthparts in 10 to 14 days.

- Mosquito bites an uninfected dog, injecting heartworm larvae into the dog's skin.
- Larvae burrow until they penetrate blood vessels and are carried to the heart and lungs. One dog may harbor as many as 250 heartworms, each up to a foot long and living 5 to 7 years. The worms initially cause inflammation of the surrounding arteries, and later, enlargement of the heart, congestive heart failure, and death.
- Adult heartworms mate and produce microfilaria that circulate in the dog's blood vessels.

veterinarians elect to omit it from the initial vaccinations. This is especially true if the dog does not walk in wooded areas or drink out of puddles where wild animals could have shed the bacteria.

Many owners of Yorkie puppies object to the idea that their tiny puppies receive the same dosage of vaccine as do large-breed puppies, and some even split the dose in half. This is not good practice. The amount of vaccine has been calculated to elicit an immune reaction, and just as infection by a virus doesn't depend on how large the dog is, neither does immunity.

Some proponents of natural rearing condemn vaccinations and refuse to use them. They use homeopathic nosodes instead, and point to the fact that their dogs don't get sick as proof that they work. However, no controlled study has ever supported the effectiveness of nosodes, and these people's good fortune is probably the result of herd immunity; that is, as long as most other dogs are vaccinated they probably never come in contact with the infectious agents.

Internal Parasite Control

Your pup should have been checked and de-wormed if necessary before coming home with you. Most pups have worms at some point because some types of worms lie dormant and protected in the dam until hormonal changes caused by her pregnancy activate them and enable them to infect her puppies. Your pup can also pick up worms from the ground in places where dogs congregate. The best prevention at home is to clean up feces immediately. Some heartworm preventives also prevent many types of worms. Get your pup regular fecal checks for worms, but don't de-worm your pup unnecessarily. Avoid over-the-counter worm medications, which are neither as safe nor effective as those available from your veterinarian.

If you see small, flat, white segments in your dog's stool, he may have tapeworms. Tapeworms are acquired when your pup eats a flea, so the best prevention is flea prevention. Special medication is required to get rid of tapeworms.

Heartworm prevention: Heartworms can kill your dog. They are carried by mosquitoes, so if there is any chance of a single mosquito biting your Yorkie, he needs to be on heartworm preventive medication. Ask your veterinarian when he should begin taking the medication, as it may vary according to your location. Dogs over 6 months of age should be checked for heartworms with a simple blood test before beginning heartworm prevention. The once-a-month preventive is safe, convenient, and effective. Treatment is available for heartworms, but it's far cheaper, easier, and safer to prevent them.

Spaying and Neutering

An intact (unspayed) female comes into estrus twice a year, usually beginning at around 8 months of age. Each heat period lasts for about three weeks, during which she will have a bloody discharge that will stain furnishings or necessitate her being crated or wearing little britches. Her scent, which she will dispense by urinating as much as possible, will advertise your home to passing males and have them whining at your door. If you have an intact male of your own, he will drive you insane with his relentless panting, whining, shaking, and clawing.

You can stop the insanity by castrating your male or spaying your female. The advantage to doing this before your dog reaches sexual maturity depends on the sex of the dog. When a male reaches sexual maturity, he starts to lift his leg when urinating in order to mark objects in his territory, which includes your furniture. He may also become more aggressive toward other dogs. The longer he does this, the more likely these behaviors are to persist after neutering.

The advantage to spaying a female before her first season is medical rather than behavioral. Spaying before her first heat season drastically reduces her chance of breast cancer in later life. Spaying before her second season helps, but not as much, and after that it has little benefit against breast cancer. Spaying at any time eliminates the possibility of pyometra, a potentially fatal infection of the uterus all too common in dogs.

The best age to castrate or spay is around 5 or 6 months. This gives your Yorkie a chance to grow, large enough to make surgery a little easier. Because it's not uncommon for Yorkies to have retained baby teeth alongside their permanent teeth, it also allows the veterinarian to remove such teeth if they don't want to fall out on their own by that age.

Chapter Five

Living With a Yorkshire Terrier

J ust as with any family member, life with your Yorkie is a blend of emotions, with times of harmony and times of head-butting. The rest of your family won't be anywhere as talented as your Yorkie is as getting their own way, of course, so there will be times you need to be tough, laugh to yourself, and just say no when it comes to his antics. Part of his advantage, besides just being so cute, is that it's often difficult to know why he's doing what he's doing. To understand that, you need to learn a little about natural dog behavior, including body language, senses, and social behavior.

Behavior Problems

Preventing and dealing with behavior problems is just as important as giving your dog vaccinations or medical treatment should he be ill. Behavior problems are the most common complaint of dog owners, and one of the most common reasons that dogs are surrendered to shelters or euthanized. And while you can't expect any dog to toe the line and never make trouble, you don't have to let such problems build until you feel there's no other choice.

Excessive Barking

Barking is second only to lack of housetraining in complaints of Yorkie owners. Barking is a natural behavior that can be traced to the Yorkie's wolf ancestry. Although adult wolves seldom bark, juvenile wolves bark as an alarm signal when intruders enter their den territory. One popular theory of dog domestication speculates that domestic dogs are neotenized wolves, meaning dogs are like wolves in various stages of arrested development. Like young wolves, adult dogs remain comparatively trustful, playful, dependent, obedient—and barky. All these traits helped them integrate more readily into human society. Barking in response to intruders was an especially valuable trait, a trait that is still valued in many dogs today. Terriers tend to be barkers, in part because the barking of a hunting terrier would alert the hunter to the dog's location, aboveground or, especially, below. Yorkies retain that tendency today.

PERSONALITY POINTERS
Yorkshire Terrier Body Language

Yorkie Mood	Playful	Interested	Confident	Submissive
Posture	Body lowered on front end only; paw placed on another dog's back; head and neck placed over another's back; shoulder or hip bump into another	Leaning forward	Leaning forward; head held high, arched neck	Leaning backward; body or head lowered and twisted; body twisted upside down; head turned away
Stance	Active, advancing	Active, stiff	Facing squarely; standing sideways	Retreating; freezing
Tail	Wagging slowly and broadly	Horizontal or natural	High	Tucked but wagging; wagging quickly and broadly
Ears	Forward or relaxed	Forward	Forward	Down
Eyes	Dilated pupils, wide	Dilated pupils	Relaxed	Turned away and squinting
Mouth	Open with lip corner pulled upward, often with tongue showing	Closed	Open or closed	Licking the air toward you or another dog; front teeth showing with no signs of aggression; muzzle push

Barking and howling also serve as auditory beacons, alerting the rest of the pack to the barker's location and drawing them all together. This is one reason a Yorkie left alone may bark and howl until the neighbors complain.

Don't get a Yorkshire Terrier, or any dog, if you demand silence. But just because it's natural doesn't mean you have to let your dog bark unchecked. Find out why he's barking, and take appropriate steps to curtail it. Many Yorkies bark simply because they are excited, perhaps announcing there's somebody at the door or, in some cases, a leaf fluttering to the ground. Here's how to teach your Yorkie a command to stop barking.

1. Don't yell at your dog to make him stop barking. He'll only think you are joining in the fun. If need be, you can throw a noisy can on the ground to distract him momentarily so he can be quiet enough to begin training.

Dominant	Aggressive	Anxious	Fearful	Pleasureable
Leaning forward with stiff-legged stance; paw placed on another dog's back; head and neck placed over another's back; shoulder or hip bump into another	Leaning forward with stiff-legged stance; paw placed on another dog's back; head and neck placed over another's back	Body or head lowered	Leaning backward; body or head lowered; body twisted upside down	Body upside down and rolling
Advancing; facing squarely	Advancing; facing squarely	Retreating	Retreating	Relaxed
Raised, held stiffly and quivering	Raised, held stiffly and quivering	Tucked	Tucked	Wagging quickly and broadly
Forward	Forward	Back	Back	
Open wide, staring	Open wide and staring; dilated pupils	Blinking rapidly	Dilated pupils	Relaxed
Closed	Agape with lip corner forward; nose or lips wrinkled, teeth showing	Licking lips; yawning; panting (may also indicate pain if not hot or tired)	Open with lip corner pulled back, all teeth showing	Open with tongue rolling

2. Wait until he is quiet momentarily and then give him a treat. This may be easier if you have him *sit* and *stay* first.
3. Keep repeating this, gradually increasing how long he must be quiet before getting a treat.
4. Add a cue word, such as "Shhhhh," as you start your timing. Eventually, he learns that "Shhhhh" means that if he is quiet he will get a treat. Remember to be calm and quiet yourself.

Not all barking stems from being overly excited. Boredom barking occurs when the dog is left alone and

has nothing else to do. Treat it by bringing him around the rest of the family. Give him interactive toys when he's isolated. Provide plenty of exercise so he's too tired to be bored.

Distress barking occurs when the dog is left alone and is distressed by his separation from you or others. This distress is often visible in other ways, such as drooling, panting, or trying to escape. It's futile to try to get him to stop barking unless you first treat him for separation distress.

Separation Distress

Separation distress is yet another problem to which many Yorkies are prone. This may be because so many Yorkies spend so much of their lives with their special people, so that a sudden departure sets off alarms.

Dogs are pack animals, and it's instinctive for them to join in whatever you or your family are doing. That means your dog is going to be unhappy shut in another room while you have company over, or left home alone when you go out. Not only is he missing out on all the fun, but, from an evolutionary viewpoint, being left alone means being put in danger.

Expert Help

Dog trainers vary widely in the level of behavioral training they provide. Look for a trainer who is a member of the Association of Pet Dog Trainers (*www.apdt.org*) and certified through the Certification Council for Pet Dog Trainers (*www.ccpdt.org*).

The Animal Behavior Society offers Applied Animal Behavior Certification for scientists and professionals in the fields of biology, psychology, animal science, and other related disciplines. They may have extensive training in neuroscience, learning, or animal behavior, but cannot prescribe drug treatments.

For serious behavior problems, a board-certified veterinary behaviorist is your best bet. Veterinary behaviorists are trained in diagnostics and treatment, and have the advantage of being able to recognize and treat organic problems such as brain tumors, epilepsy, and chemical imbalances that may be responsible for behavior problems. They are keen observers of behavior, and may spot clues that you have either missed or misinterpreted. Your veterinarian can consult with one or refer you to one in your area (go to *www.veterinarybehaviorists.org* for a listing).

Under natural circumstances, separation from the dam and littermates would be a dangerous situation. As the puppies grow older, they are gradually introduced to more separation time. In domestic dogs, it's more often an abrupt process, usually beginning when the puppy goes to his new home. The dog can become scared very easily when first left alone, and can quickly come to expect to feel afraid when left alone. When that happens, the situation builds on itself and works up to full-blown separation distress.

Signs of a dog with separation distress include whining, howling, barking, panting, drooling, pacing, and digging and chewing at doors and windows while you're gone. The dog may also urinate and defecate on the floor or in

the crate. Many people think the dog is spiting them, but dogs never destroy out of spite. That fact that your dog may look guilty when you come home usually stems from past experiences with what seems to him to be your irrational homecoming behavior. Here he is finally reunited with you, and you start acting crazy. He learns to act submissive when you return home, especially if the house just happens to be in a shambles.

If you're still not convinced, set up a video camera and watch him while you're gone. You won't see a dog gleefully venting his anger on your home. You'll see a dog who is upset and perhaps near panicked. This is not a dog who needs to be punished; he's a dog who needs to be helped.

Shutting the dog in a crate or pen doesn't fix the problem, but only confines it. And ignoring the dog for long periods doesn't help, because it doesn't teach the dog not to be upset. The best time to deal with separation distress is before it ever happens, when your dog is a puppy. Begin by leaving him for very short periods, perhaps with a special treat or interactive toy, and gradually lengthening it. Remember, your goal is to never let him become distressed, rather than having to deal with fixing the problem later.

If you do have a dog with separation distress, consult your veterinarian or better yet, a veterinary behaviorist to deal with the problem. It can be fixed, but the sooner you start, the easier it will be. Start with these steps.

Graduate departures. Leave for only short periods to begin with—maybe 30 seconds at first. Your goal is to return before your dog has a chance to get upset. Work up to longer times gradually, repeating each level several times before moving to a longer period of absence.

Use a safety cue. When first training with short periods, give your dog a cue that says to him, "I'll be right back." You can spray some air freshener in the room, turn on a radio (if you don't usually have one on), or put down a special bed. You want him to associate the safety cue with feeling calm. If you must be gone longer than your dog can tolerate, don't give him the safety cue.

Downplay departures. Except for the safety cue, minimize any other cues that you're leaving. Don't turn the radio or television on or off reliably, don't rattle keys, don't put your shoes on right before you leave, and don't have any big good-bye scenes.

Downplay returns. Just as you downplayed your departure, return as though it were no big deal. That means no crazed reunions. Ignore your dog until he is calm, or better, give him a cue to sit or do some other behavior involving self control, and then reward him for that.

Consider anti-anxiety aids. Many dogs may not be calm enough in your absence to make much progress. The use of dog-appeasing pheromones, which are odors that mimic the calming scent of a lactating dam, has been shown to help some dogs. They are available from pet stores as a spray or room plug-in.

Tough cases may benefit from anti-anxiety drugs. As with all drug therapy, this is not something you decide to do on your own, but rather should be undertaken under the guidance of a veterinary behaviorist.

Biting

Yorkies get away with a lot of bad behavior, but biting is one you cannot excuse. Yet, too many Yorkie owners do so, either because they figure he really can't do much damage, or that it's cute, or because they're afraid to stand up to their dogs! Allowing your Yorkie to bite not only makes him very unpopular, but it could set you up for a lawsuit and him up for being impounded or labeled a dangerous dog.

Although you can't afford to tolerate any biting, not all biting is created equal. Biting done in play is different from biting done in fear, and both are

BE PREPARED! Recognizing the Bite

Playful biting	Fearful biting	Aggressive biting
Wagging tail	Tucked tail	Stiffly held tail
Bowing position	Crouched position	Stiff, tip-toe position
Running and bouncing	Slinking or cornered	Standing or charging
Barks and growls together	Whines and growls	Low growl, perhaps barks
Breathy exhale sounds	No exhale sounds	No exhale sounds
Mouthing	No mouthing	No mouthing
Eye contact	Looks away	Eye contact
Licks at you	Licks own lips	No licking
Lip corner pulled upward	Lip corner pulled back	Lip corner pulled forward
Repeated nips or grabs	Sudden bite, then retreat	Sudden, hard bites

different from biting done as a challenge or while guarding a resource. Each must be dealt with differently, so the first thing you must do is learn to tell one type of biting from another.

Playful biting. Playful biting is normal for puppies and does not indicate that your puppy is going to grow into a bad dog. But it still hurts, and you don't want to encourage it. Instead, when your puppy grabs you, say "Ouch! No!" and remove your hand. Substitute a toy. If the puppy continues, just stand there and ignore him. He'll soon learn that when he plays too rough, you don't want to play with him anymore.

Fearful biting. Fearful biting occurs when a dog is placed in a fight-or-flight situation and can't flee. In Yorkies, it often occurs when a dog that's afraid of strangers is forced to allow a stranger to pet or hold him. Unable to get away, the dog finally lashes out at the approaching stranger. Don't expect your Yorkie to be held by a stranger unless he's comfortable with it, and if you do hand your dog over, hand him rear-first, rather than face-first, which reduces the inclination and ability to bite.

Fear biting can also occur when a dog has been punished severely and the owner swoops down to grab him, especially if the dog is cornered. The dog may have found that warning growls or bites make the threatening person stop, which teaches the dog that such behavior is rewarding.

Treatment should center around helping the dog overcome his fears. Meanwhile, take the following precautions:

- Do not place a fear-aggressive dog in situations that could cause him to be afraid.
- Do not punish a fear-aggressive dog for his behavior. It only makes things worse because it verifies his fears.

- Do not force a fear-aggressive dog to face his fears, and do not corner or reach for him. These situations greatly increase the chance that he may bite, which in turn becomes self-perpetuating. Instead, call the dog to you and have him act calm or do a trick for a reward.
- Do not reassure or pet a fear-aggressive dog while he is acting inappropriately. This gives the dog the message that he is acting appropriately.

Aggressive biting. Aggressive biting can mean that your dog is guarding territory or belongings, or that he is challenging you. Like most terriers, Yorkies tend to be territorial, and many don't hesitate to protect their homes and yards from intruders, even if they're invited guests.

Treat territorial aggression by removing the possibility that your dog will encounter somebody from whom to protect his territory. That means removing him from the fenced yard when passersby are expected, and from the front door area when company is coming. He should be rewarded for sitting and staying when strangers arrive, and gradually moved closer to them. You can eventually have visitors bring him treats.

Some Yorkies guard their food or toys. Unfortunately, some owners unwittingly create this behavior by repeatedly taking the dog's food away to teach him to tolerate it. The only thing this accomplishes is to teach the dog that his food is, indeed, in danger. A better scheme is to convince the dog that hands

CAUTION

How NOT to Correct an Aggressive Yorkshire Terrier

You may have heard the following methods suggested as means of asserting your dominance over your dog. Do not use them. They have been shown to be ineffective, unsafe, and based on faulty interpretations of wolf pack behavior.

- **Myth:** "Scruff shakes are good corrections because they mimic the way a mother dog corrects her puppies." No! Mother dogs rarely, if ever, correct their pups by scruff shaking (shaking by the scruff of the neck). Scruff shaking can lead to neck injuries, and is especially foolish in tiny dogs.
- **Myth:** "Alpha rolls are good corrections because they mimic the way a dominant dog exerts its dominance over a subordinate dog." No! "Alpha roll" is the term used to describe the act of forcing a dog on his back and holding him there until he stops struggling. At one time it was thought this was how high-ranking wolves exerted their dominance over low-ranking pack members. But now it's known that dominant dogs exert most of their dominance simply by ignoring subordinates. When subordinates roll on their backs in front of dominant wolves or dogs, the subordinates do it themselves; they are never forced. Alpha rolls conducted by humans in attempts to subdue already challenging dogs often result in dog bites.

near his food are bringers, not takers, of food. As he is eating, drop special treats into his bowl. If you must take his bowl away, substitute another bowl with some treats in it. The same is true with toys. If you must take one away, replace it with another.

Some Yorkies seem to get a kick out of preventing people from getting on the bed or other furniture. It may start as a game or be part of territorial behavior. An easy solution is to fold your arms and back toward the furniture under dispute. He will probably find the game is no fun and quit his behavior. If he persists, or if he refuses to get off furniture when you tell him to, have him wear a short leash around the house so you can pull him down without having a hands-on confrontation.

If your dog continues to challenge your authority, establish your position by remaining somewhat aloof and not allowing him to take liberties with you, such as pulling you around, jumping on you, or demanding food or petting when he feels like it. Be a leader by engaging him in cooperative activities such as walks and training games. Don't fawn on him, even though you love him. Fawning is what subordinates do. You want your Yorkie to fawn on you, and one way that might help bring him around is to ignore him for several days. Make him earn your attention, even his food, by doing a simple trick, such as sitting, when you ask.

Mounting

Mounting, or humping, can become a problem in some Yorkies. Although more common in intact males, even females and neutered males can mount excessively. Adults may mount one another as a sign of dominance. Females in heat often mount one another. Males around females in heat will also mount each other and, in some cases, you or anything else they can wrap their paws around.

Puppies mount other puppies as part of their regular play, and without another puppy around they may try to mount some part of you. If they are mounting another puppy just ignore it; it's normal. But if your puppy tries to mount your leg, simply peel him off and distract him with a toy or another activity. If he persists, tell him "No" firmly and, if need be, separate him until he can mind his manners.

The same is true if your adult, tries to mount your leg, only in this case you can be more firm. This is not a cute behavior that should ever be encouraged because it tends to be self-gratifying and the dog will tend to repeat it. However, do not overreact and kick the dog off; he does not understand our society's view of such behavior.

Some male Yorkies will mount a stuffed animal or a pillow, and follow through until they ejaculate. Again, this should be discouraged because some dogs become obsessed with this sexual self-gratification. Remove favored target items and distract your dog with games and plenty of exercise. If you have an intact male, consider neutering him. The earlier this is done the less likely the behavior will persist after neutering.

Chewing

Puppies explore with their mouths, carrying, licking, grabbing, biting, and gnawing anything they can reach, practicing skills they will need as adults. Such practice does not make for happy discoveries, though, when you find your new shoes and antique furniture riddled with pinprick teeth punctures.

The best defense is to keep everything chewable out of reach, and never let your puppy loose in the house unsupervised. Inundate him with acceptable chew toys, especially interactive ones. And keep him well exercised so he'd rather sleep than explore when you're at home. The same is true of adults that chew. Don't expect your Yorkie to miraculously stop chewing on his first birthday. It will be a few more years before you can leave him amongst your treasures and expect all to be intact upon your return.

Fearful Behavior

Yorkies can be the little Napoleons of the dog world, but even so, they can develop irrational fears, most often of strange people, strange dogs, or thunder. First, here's what not to do:

- Don't make a big deal of the situation. This only reinforces the idea that there's something to be afraid of. Instead, put on your party face and act like all is well.
- Don't immerse your fearful Yorkie in the frightening situation. Long ago, people thought, when someone was afraid of something, that if you flooded them with exposure to the feared thing they'd get over it. It didn't work in people, no more than hanging you off a building would cure your fear of heights, or piling your bed with snakes would cure you of your fear of snakes. But for some reason, people, even dog trainers, still advocate the idea for dogs. Don't do it. If your Yorkie is afraid of people, having a roomful of people converge on him to pet him will only make him more fearful, not less. If he's afraid of thunder, putting him outside during an electrical storm will only increase his fear, not diminish it.
- Don't punish your fearful Yorkie. He's doing the best he can.
- Don't reward your fearful Yorkie with treats and petting. You don't want to reinforce his fearful behavior.

Instead, you need to help your dog build his confidence and feeling of control when around a fear-provoking situation. You do this by combining several behavioral techniques. The same concepts apply whether your Yorkie is afraid of people, dogs, or loud noises. If you don't seem to be making progress, consult a veterinary behaviorist, who may prescribe antianxiety drugs to help in the initial phases of training.

Gradual desensitization. Start each session at a level that may cause some anxiety to your dog, but not so much that he is still as fearful at the end of the session. This may mean having a stranger walk within a few feet of him and ignore him at first. Remember, your dog is learning to be calm. If he's still afraid at the end of a session, all you have taught him is how to be scared.

Give some control. Give your dog some control. Studies have shown that dogs that have some control over a situation adjust to it better than those that don't. Instead of holding your dog in place, or letting him drag you away from a scary person, for example, have him sit when the person is near, and as a reward for sitting, allow him to move farther away and sit again. Gradually extend how long he has to sit, or how close the person gets to be.

Counter-conditioning. Getting your dog to do something incompatible with fear, such as relaxing, eating, playing, hunting, or walking, will help him associate good things and good feelings with the feared object. For instance, taking your dog for a walk with another person is more helpful than meeting a stranger at a shopping center. You can have somebody visit while you massage your dog, or feed him in the presence of strangers.

Imitation. Your dog won't be helped if he sees other dogs (or people) acting fearful, but he might be encouraged to join in if his best doggy friend is getting petted by and eating treats from somebody else.

Lack of Housetraining

The most common serious complaint of Yorkie owners is lack of housetraining. In fact, toy breeds in general are notorious for being difficult to housetrain. Some people theorize that the small bladders of toy dogs makes it difficult for them to hold their urine for very long, or that they simply have less bladder control. Others attribute it to early experiences. Many toy dogs are raised in pens indoors, so they aren't exposed to eliminating outside. Dogs that are raised in pens where they're forced to relieve themselves inside tend to be indiscriminate about where they go in later life. In fact, as adults, dogs tend to prefer using the same type of surface they eliminated on as puppies. That means you need to decide where you want your dog to eliminate as an adult, and start using that same surface area while he's a puppy—even if it means hauling sod squares inside the house during bad weather. And you have to be consistent and watchful. You can't put off going to the potty area because the weather's bad or you're in a hurry. You can't decide to just let the puppy relieve himself inside because it's easy to sop up off the tile. You can't make exceptions; you can't be inconsistent.

If your adult Yorkie doesn't seem to care where he eliminates, you need to start from scratch and housetrain him as though he were a puppy learning it for the first time. Another option is to compromise with an indoor potty system (see page 51).

Physical Causes of Housetraining Woes

If remedial housetraining still doesn't work, especially if he used to be housetrained, consider the possibility of a physical problem. Physical problems include:

- Urinary tract infections. These cause repeated urges to urinate with little warning.
- Diabetes and kidney disease. These cause increased drinking along with increased urination.
- Some drugs, such as steroids. These cause increased drinking and urination.
- Urinary incontinence. This is more likely in spayed females.
- Age-related cognitive problems. Geriatric dogs may forget their house manners and have accidents.
- Internal parasites, gastrointestinal upsets, and some food allergies. These can cause uncontrollable diarrhea.

A veterinary exam is warranted in any case of housetraining failure. If a physical problem is the cause, once the problem is cured you may still have to start all over with remedial lessons. If the problem can't be cured, you may need to make compromises with absorbent bed pads, doggy diapers, or waterproof flooring.

Involuntary emissions. Does your Yorkie tend to urinate when you bend over to greet him or perhaps when he's dancing around in excitement as you come home? This is classic submissive urination. He can't help it, and punishing him will only make it worse because he'll be more submissive. Submissive urination occurs in both sexes, but is more common in females than males. The good news is that most dogs will probably outgrow it, specially if you help build their confidence and take care not to intimidate them. That means you avoid bending over him, staring at him, scolding him, or otherwise intimidating him when you don't want him to urinate. Keep your greetings calm, get down on his level, and ignore him if he urinates. By teaching him a few tricks you can increase his confidence and give him a way to earn rewards.

Some dogs just can't help dribbling urine when they're excited. They, too, will usually outgrow this excitement urination as they gain bladder control. The best treatment is to decrease the excitement level. If possible, gradually condition your dog to be calm during low excitement events, working up gradually to higher excitement events. Teach some simple low-key tricks to distract and calm him. Punishing a dog with excitement urination will only lead to confusion and possibly submissive urination. In either case, it makes sense to greet your dog outdoors or on an easily cleaned surface!

Bad boys. Males that urinate in the house by lifting their legs on furniture or walls aren't doing it because they just have to go. They're doing it because they just have to mark. Urine marking is a natural behavior of adult dogs in which they squirt urine to claim their territory. Because it's so much a part of a mature male's behavioral repertoire, marking is hard to break. Sometimes the behavior begins when another male visits or if a female in estrus comes around. Diligent deodorizing can help, but the most effective cure is neutering. Even that's not a guarantee, especially if he's already been urine marking for a while. If he has favorite marking places, try feeding him or making him sleep in those areas, since dogs don't like to mark so close to their eating and sleeping quarters.

Incorrigible males can wear a belly-band indoors. Think of it as a diaper for bad boys. It's a band of material that wraps around the dog's midriff. The band holds an absorbent pad in the crucial location so, when the dog lifts his leg, the urine is caught by the pad. Belly-bands are available at most pet supply stores and over the Internet.

Communicating with Your Yorkshire Terrier

Scent Yorkies may not be known as hunters or trackers, or even contraband detectors, but they can be trained to do any of those jobs. They can detect a particular component of human skin scent one hundred million times better than you can. They also detect crushed vegetation and stirred-up dirt from each footstep.

You'll often see your Yorkie use his sense of smell in social interactions. Dogs get to know each other by first sniffing at each others genitals, anus, mouth corners, and ears, all areas that produce a good deal of scent.

As much as you may protest that your Yorkie doesn't have any doggy smell, all dogs communicate by leaving powerful scent signals through anal sac secretions. When dogs are extremely frightened, they expel their anal sacs to produce a strong musky smell that instantly elicits intense interest from other dogs, perhaps telling them that something terrifying happened there.

People don't tend to use scent much when communicating with each other or with dogs. However, if you're scared or stressed, your body produces adrenaline and also tends to sweat more, which may cause differences in your odor that your Yorkie can perceive.

Hearing If your Yorkie cocks his head, looks at the window at night, and starts growling, pay attention. He can hear a lot better than you can. He can hear mid-range noises about four times farther away than you can, and high-pitched sounds you can't hear at any distance. The lowest-pitched sounds that dogs and people can hear are about the same, around 45 to 65 hertz (Hz). However, people hear sounds of around 3,000 Hz most easily (most people's voices are near that frequency), but dogs are most sensitive to higher-pitched sounds of around 8,000 Hz. That's why he can hear dog whistles and you can't.

You don't have to shout at your dog, or even talk in a high-pitched voice, for him to hear you, although in an old dog with hearing loss, using a loud, low-pitched voice may help. Be consistent in the words you use and the way you say them. Dogs hear your words as sounds, not as vowels and consonants that mean the same thing no matter how they are said. When talking to your dog, teach commands in a normal voice, and just say them once. Shouting or repeating won't help your dog understand a command. Use low-pitched sounds to make your dog stop doing something. They indicate power, aggression, and leadership, and are often used as threats. Use high-pitched sounds to encourage your dog to interact or play. Long, drawn-out, monotone speech will slow or calm your dog. Use abrupt, low-pitched commands to stop your dog. A series of repeated short, high-pitched sounds that continue to rise in pitch will hurry a dog.

Vision

Dogs have color vision like people who are typical red-green colorblind; that is, they can tell blue from yellow but confuse reds, oranges, yellows, and greens. Even though dogs do see colors, they don't seem to pay a lot of attention to them. But dogs have an advantage over people when it comes to seeing in dim light. Their greater proportion of rod to cone visual receptors allows them to run in the dark without tripping. Dogs are also adept at discerning slight movements, which is why your Yorkie is able to read subtle changes in your facial expressions and body positions. They don't have great detail vision, however, so they can actually have difficulty recognizing you just from sight unless you move or talk or get close enough to scent.

Domestic dogs are one of the few non-human animals that can interpret the meaning of a human pointing or looking at something. They are actually aware of your eye position and can use it to cue on where you have something hidden, for example. They can also wait until your eyes are closed or your back is turned to snatch some forbidden food, showing they understand what eyes are there for!

Taste

Yorkies pride themselves on their discriminating taste, but they still manage to eat some things that strike us as unsavory. Dogs and humans have different taste receptors and different senses of taste. Compared to people, the greatest anatomical difference is the dog's lack of strong salt-specific taste buds. And while dogs enjoy sweets, they don't like saccharin, probably because it's been shown that their taste buds respond more to the bitter aftertaste than they do to any sweet aspect.

Touch

Puppies grow up needing to be touched by their dam and littermates, especially when sleeping, and this trait often remains throughout life. Yorkies thrive on being touched and petted, and yours may shove his head under your hand to remind you of your duties if you're negligent. When adult dogs are petted, their heart and breathing rates decrease and they appear calmer. The best way to calm a dog through petting is to use deep muscle massage with long, firm strokes reaching from the head to the rear. Petting a dog has also been shown to calm people and lower their blood pressure.

Most dogs don't actually enjoyed being hugged because, in dogdom, the hugger is usually showing his dominance in the form of mounting the huggee. But dogs do enjoy being held or allowed to snuggle close when resting.

Chapter Six

Health and Nutrition

our Yorkie depends on you to help him live a comfortable life as free of illness and pain as possible. In most cases, this responsibility is fairly simple to live up to: Basic vaccinations and nutrition, along with annual checkups, seem to do the job. But in other cases, your Yorkie may require more extensive veterinary care or a special diet. This is part of the commitment you made when you adopted him as a family member. Don't let him down.

Veterinary Care and Choices

Your choice of veterinarian is one of the most important decisions you will make for your Yorkie. Consider availability, emergency arrangements, facilities, costs, ability to communicate, interaction with your dog, and experience with Yorkies when making your decision. All veterinary practices have pros and cons. A practice with several veterinarians can often provide more services than one with a single veterinarian, but it may not have the personal approach. Some practices may have state-of-the-art technology, but if you can't afford to go there, it doesn't do much good.

Most veterinarians in general practice can provide a wide range of services, but if your dog has a problem that eludes diagnosis or requires specialized treatment, let your veterinarian know if you

Breed Needs

Health Insurance

As veterinary medicine has become more sophisticated, it's also become more expensive, which has brought about pet health insurance. Pet health policies have annual premiums and offer different deductibles and coverage plans. The premiums depend in part on the dog's age and any preexisting conditions. Make sure that any plan you consider does not exclude hereditary conditions commonly seen in Yorkies such as portosystemic (liver) shunts and patellar luxation. Some plans cover routine care whereas others cover only illness or injury. Your own veterinarian may offer wellness packages.

FYI: Worrisome Changes in Appearance or Behavior

These signs . . .	may indicate (among other causes) . . .
Lethargic, lying in a curled position	Fever, general illness, weakness
Irritability, restlessness	Pain
Clawing, panting, trembling, hiding	Pain, fear
Repeated stretching and bowing	Abdominal pain
Restlessness, retching, bowing	**Gut obstruction/Bloat—EMERGENCY**
Pain when lifted	Back or neck pain, disc disease
Refusal to lie down	Breathing problems, abdominal pain
Refusal to put head down	Breathing problems, neck pain
Head-pressing, seizures	Neurological problems, liver shunt
Weakness, pale gums	Illness, internal bleeding, anemia
Dizziness, head tilt	Vestibular disease, ear infection
Loss of appetite	Illness, fever, kidney disease
Increased appetite	Cushing's syndrome, diabetes
Increased thirst (and urination)	Diabetes, kidney disease, Cushing's syndrome
Frequent, sudden, painful urination	Urinary tract infection
Difficult, painful urination; bloody urine	Kidney or bladder stones
Inability to urinate	**Blockage—EMERGENCY**
Regurgitating food right after eating	Esophageal/swallowing problem
Vomiting	Illness, poisoning, blockage, other
Coughing	Kennel cough, heart disease, tracheal collapse
Gagging (chronic)	Tracheal collapse, laryngeal paralysis, foreign body
Enlarged abdomen, progressive	Cushing's syndrome, pregnancy, pyometra, heart failure
Enlarged abdomen, sudden	**Bloat, internal bleeding—EMERGENCY**

are willing to be referred to a specialist. Such specialists can be found at veterinary schools and in private practices in larger cities, but expect to pay much higher fees to see one.

Common Tests and Procedures

Besides going to the veterinarian when he's sick, your Yorkie needs an annual wellness examination. Because dogs age faster than humans, a yearly physical in a dog is like a person only having one every five years or so, and some veterinarians even advocate twice-yearly exams.

Wellness exams. A wellness exam typically consists of examining the mouth, teeth, eyes, ears, and genitals; listening to the heart and lungs; feeling

along the spine; pressing against the abdomen in order to feel the internal organs; and very likely drawing blood for a heartworm test and getting a stool sample to check for worms or their eggs. Some veterinarians also draw a blood sample so that they have baseline values for your dog to compare to later samples should he ever become sick. In addition, the veterinarian may check a sample for indications of liver shunt (see page 102).

If your Yorkie is ill, the veterinarian will perform many of these same exams, depending on the nature of the illness, and may also perform some specialized tests.

Blood tests. Some of the most common, and informative, tests your veterinarian may perform are blood tests, which include a complete blood count (CBC) and perhaps a serum chemistry profile. The CBC checks red and white blood cells, and can identify

(see page 102)

CAUTION

Gum Color

Your Yorkie's gum color is the window to his blood, and should be one of the first things you check when you suspect illness. Gums should be a deep pink, and if you press them with your thumb, they should return to pink within 2 seconds after lifting your thumb (a longer time suggests a circulatory problem).

Gum color . . .	could mean . . .
Pale or white	Anemia, shock, internal bleeding
Bluish	Lack of oxygen, poor circulation
Bright red	Overheating, carbon monoxide poisoning
Brick red	High fever
Yellowish	Liver disease
Red splotches	Blood clotting problem

CHECKLIST

The Home Checkup

Make several copies of this checklist and keep a record of your dog's home check-ups. Check the following:

Weight: ☐ Increased? ☐ Decreased?

Mouth: ☐ Loose teeth? ☐ Painful? ☐ Dirty? ☐ Bad breath?

Gums: ☐ Swellings? ☐ Bleeding? ☐ Sores? ☐ Growths?

Gum color: ☐ Pink (good) ☐ Bright red ☐ Bluish ☐ Whitish ☐ Red spots

Nose: ☐ Thick or colored discharge? ☐ Cracking? ☐ Pinched? ☐ Sores?

Eyes: ☐ Tearing? ☐ Mucous discharge? ☐ Dull surface? ☐ Squinting? ☐ Swelling? ☐ Redness? ☐ Unequal pupils? ☐ Pawing at eyes?

Ears: ☐ Bad smell? ☐ Redness? ☐ Abundant debris? ☐ Scabby ear tips? ☐ Head shaking? ☐ Head tilt? ☐ Ear scratching? ☐ Painfulness?

Legs: ☐ Asymmetrical bones or muscles? ☐ Lumps? ☐ Weakness? ☐ Limping?

Feet: ☐ Long or split nails? ☐ Cut pads? ☐ Swollen or misaligned toes?

Skin: ☐ Parasites? ☐ Black grains (flea dirt)? ☐ Hair loss? ☐ Scabs? ☐ Greasy patches? ☐ Bad odor? ☐ Lumps?

Abdomen: ☐ Bloated? ☐ Pendulous? ☐ Painful?

Anal and genital regions: ☐ Swelling? ☐ Discharge? ☐ Redness? ☐ Bloody urine? ☐ Bloody or blackened diarrhea? ☐ Worms in stool or around anus? ☐ Scooting rear? ☐ Licking rear?

Tail: ☐ Limp?

If you answered "yes" to anything abnormal on the checklist, contact your veterinarian for advice.

problems such as anemia, leukemia, and the presence of many infections. A serum chemistry profile provides information on how various organs are functioning. Within minutes, the results can tell you if your dog feels ill because of kidney failure, liver disease, or pancreatitis, for example, enabling the veterinarian to start treatment immediately.

Problem Signs

Your veterinarian may use sophisticated tests to detect and diagnose health problems, but you have an even more powerful weapon: the knowledge of what's normal for your dog, and the awareness of signs he's not feeling well.

Note that many other problems can cause these signs, and you should always consult your veterinarian as soon as possible for a diagnosis and treatment.

Lethargy

Lethargy is the most common sign of illness. Possible causes include:

- Infection (check for fever),
- Anemia (check gum color),
- Circulatory problem (check pulse and gum color),
- Pain (check limbs, neck, back, mouth, eyes, ears, and abdomen for signs),
- Liver shunt (see page 102),
- Nausea,
- Poisoning (check gum color and pupil reaction; look for vomiting or abdominal pain),
- Sudden vision loss,
- Cancer, and
- Metabolic diseases.

High or Low Temperature

A high temperature can make your Yorkie feel bad, and could indicate that a trip to the veterinarian is needed. To take your Yorkie's temperature, lubricate a rectal thermometer and insert it about 2 inches (5 cm) into his anus, leaving it there for about a minute. Normal is from 101 to 102°F (38.3 to 38.9°C). If the temperature is:

- 103°F (39.4°C) or above, call your veterinarian for advice. Of itself, this is not usually an emergency, but it is a concern.
- 104°F (40°C) or above, go to your veterinarian. This is probably an emergency; 105°F or above is definitely an emergency. Meanwhile, try to cool your dog by dampening his skin and placing him in front of a fan. Do not dunk him in icy water, which constricts surface vessels and traps the hot temperature at the body core.
- 98°F (36.6°C) or below, call your veterinarian for advice. Try to warm your dog.
- 97°F (36.1°C) or below, go to your veterinarian. Treat for hypothermia on the way by warming your dog with hot water bottles, blankets, or your own body.

Diarrhea

Diarrhea can result from nervousness, a change in diet or water, food sensitivities, intestinal parasites, infections, poisoning, or many illnesses. It's not uncommon for dogs to have blood in their diarrhea, but diarrhea with lots of blood, or accompanied by vomiting, fever, or other symptoms of illness, warrants a call to the veterinarian. Bright-red blood indicates a source lower in the digestive tract, while dark-black, tarry stools indicate a source higher in the digestive tract. In most dogs, the best treatment is to withhold food for 24 hours, and then feed rice and low-fat foods. But in small Yorkies, especially puppies, the possibility of hypoglycemia precludes this, so you must instead feed small low-fat meals. Ask your veterinarian about using anti-diarrhea medication.

Helpful Hints

Scooting

If your Yorkie scoots his rear on the ground, he may have worms, but he more likely has impacted anal sacs. The anal sacs are small sacs filled with pungent material, located just inside the anus. A bit of the material is normally secreted each time the dog defecates or if he's very frightened, but in some, especially small dogs, the opening becomes clogged and the material builds up inside, where it stretches the sac and hurts. In some cases the sacs are stretched so much they rupture, creating a hole to the outside of the dog just beside the anus. A veterinarian or groomer can express the sacs for you and relieve the pain. You can also learn to do it yourself. In some cases, the sacs will become infected, which requires veterinary treatment.

Breed Truths

Breed Predispositions

The following disorders, although not considered major concerns in the breed, are seen in Yorkies at frequencies somewhat higher than in many other breeds.

- Atlantoaxial subluxation (misalignment of the first two neck vertebrae, causing pain and spinal cord problems)
- Cataracts (loss of transparency of the lens of the eye)
- Cryptorchidism (failure of one or both testicles to descend into the scrotum)
- Distichiasis (extra eyelashes that may grow toward and irritate the eye)
- Eclampsia (calcium depletion of the dam when nursing)
- Entropion (inward-turned eyelid, so that lashes irritate the eye surface)
- Hemorrhagic gastroenteritis (sudden bloody diarrhea that may require hospitalization to combat dehydration)
- Hepatic lipidosis (fatty liver disease; the accumulation of excessive amounts of fat within liver cells)
- Hydrocephalus (excessive accumulation of cerebrospinal fluid within the brain, leading to mental slowness)
- Hypoglycemia (low blood sugar leading to neurological signs)
- Hypoplasia of dens (misalignment of the first two neck bones, leading to pain and sometimes paralysis)
- Keratoconjunctivitis sicca (decreased tear production, leading to dry eye and irritation of the eye surface)
- Patent ductus arteriosus (congenital heart defect)
- Progressive retinal degeneration (degeneration of light-sensitive cells in the retina, leading to blindness)
- Urolithiasis (bladder stones)

Yorkshire Terrier Special Concerns

Every breed of dog has its own set of hereditary headaches when it comes to health problems. In some cases, these problems became prevalent in the breed because one or more of the founding dogs happened to have the genes for that problem, and because of the closed gene pool that is a breed, those genes became widespread. In other cases, the problem is a secondary effect of some aspect of the dog's desired conformation.

In Yorkies, the breed-associated disorders that are of most concern, aside from hypoglycemia (see page 61), are liver shunt, tracheal collapse, patellar luxation, and Legg-Calvé-Perthes disease.

Tracheal collapse. Tracheal collapse is most common in toy breeds, including Yorkies. Affected dogs often cough with a harsh "goose-honk," especially when excited, when pressure is put on the throat, or when eating or drinking. In severe cases, the dog can't get enough air, and may faint or get a bluish cast to the tongue.

The trachea, or windpipe, is made up of a series of cartilage rings. In some Yorkies, the cartilage isn't as rigid as it should be, and some of the rings collapse, flattening the trachea and obstructing breathing. If the collapse is in the neck area, the dog has trouble inhaling. If the collapse is in the chest area, the dog has trouble exhaling.

Several factors can make collapse of a weakened ring more likely. Obesity, respiratory infection, enlarged heart, endotracheal intubation, or inhalation of irritants or allergens can all bring on an episode. Coughing, which is a major symptom, can also worsen the condition.

The best way to diagnose the condition is with an endoscope, which usually means going to an internal medicine specialist. Your own veterinarian may be able to take a series of radiographs (X-rays) to diagnose the condition. The trachea changes its dimensions as the dog breathes in and out, so a single radiograph often misses the critical time.

In severe cases, surgery, in which prosthetic supports are implanted, may be the best option. This must be done by a specialist who has experience in this type of surgery, because it's not always successful.

In less severe cases, reducing weight, using a harness instead of a collar, humidifying the air, avoiding irritants such as cigarette smoke, and avoiding any situation that could lead to overheating, stress, heavy panting, or coughing can help. Glucosamine and vitamin C supplements may help strengthen cartilage. Bronchodilators may be helpful at times, but their use is controversial.

Patellar luxation. Patellar luxation is a common problem of smaller dogs, including Yorkies. It involves the patella, or kneecap, of one or both rear legs. Normally, the patella slides up and down in a small groove of the femur (thigh bone) as the leg bends and the knee moves. If the groove is too shallow, though, the patella can ride over the side of the groove. This can also happen if the tendon of the quadriceps muscle has too much rotational pull.

Once out of place (the technical term for this is *luxated*), the muscle has to relax before the patella can pop back into place. Relaxing the muscle means the leg must be straightened at the knee, so the dog will often hop for a few steps with the leg held straight until the patella pops back. Suspect patellar luxation if your Yorkie occasionally holds one hind leg up and forward. He may also yelp, because it hurts when it rides back over the ridge. It also wears down the ridge, causing the condition to get gradually worse.

Patellar luxation can affect one or both legs. The patella may slip toward either side, but in small dogs it's usually toward the inside, which gives the dog a bowlegged look.

Signs are usually apparent by 6 months of age. Early diagnosis is helpful in slowing the progress, but treatment depends on what grade of severity it is.

- **Grade 1:** The dog may occasionally skip, keeping one hind leg up and straight for a step or two. The patella can be pushed out of position by hand but returns to its correct position easily.
- **Grade 2:** The dog often holds the affected leg up and straight when moving. The patella may not slide back into position by itself.
- **Grade 3:** The dog only sometimes uses the affected leg. The patella is usually out of position, slipping back out almost as soon as it is replaced.
- **Grade 4:** The dog never puts weight on the leg. The patella is always out of position and cannot be replaced manually.

Signs can appear as early as 8 weeks of age. Cases that appear in puppyhood usually develop into grade 3 or 4 in adulthood. Cases that first appear in young adults usually develop into grade 2 or 3. Cases that first appear in older adults are usually grade 1 or 2.

Surgery to tighten any stretched tissues and reconstruct the groove or realign the muscle will improve the condition. However, in an older dog with grade 1 or 2, it may not be necessary. A young dog with grade 1 or 2, or any age dog with grade 3 or 4, is a candidate. Surgery may not make the leg perfect, but it will enable your Yorkie to run and walk relatively pain-free. An orthopedic specialist has the best chance of success.

Legg-Calvé-Perthes disease. Legg-Calvé-Perthes disease is a disease of the hip joints that occurs when the head of the femur (the ball part of the ball and socket) loses its blood supply and deteriorates, causing limping and pain. It often occurs only in one leg.

The first signs usually appear in late puppyhood. In some dogs, signs are subtle and no treatment is needed, whereas in others it causes significant pain. Diagnosis can be made with an X-ray. Treatment for severe cases is with surgery, in which the femur head is removed. The muscles then form a false joint, which works well in small dogs.

Lymphangiectasia.
Lymphangiectasia is a condition in which lymph fluid, which is normally collected from tissues and returned to the blood, instead is blocked so that intestinal lymph leaks into the intestines, where it is lost in the stool. This causes a loss of essential lymph components including protein, white blood cells,

and fats. This is turn can cause weight loss or stunted growth, as well as swollen legs and abdomen. The dog may also have persistent but mild diarrhea. Some dogs have trouble breathing. Diagnosis is with various laboratory tests and an intestinal biopsy. Lymphangiectasia can't be cured, but it can be managed through diet and medication. The diet should contain minimal levels of fat and high levels of high-quality protein. Corticosteriods may be given to reduce intestinal inflammation.

Yorkies and Dental Problems

Like most small dogs, Yorkies have a high incidence of dental disease. In fact, according to one study, tooth and gum problems are the most common reason Yorkies of all ages are taken to the veterinarian. Small breeds have comparatively less jawbone density to support their teeth compared to large breeds, and Yorkies have low jawbone density compared to other small breeds. In addition, Yorkie teeth are comparatively large for their mouths, and can be crowded or have somewhat shallow roots.

Crowded teeth can sometimes affect occlusion, which is important for good dental health. In correct Yorkshire Terrier occlusion, the top incisors (the little front teeth) fit just in front of the bottom ones. Many Yorkies start losing their adult teeth at a very early age. The problem starts with plaque, which leads to tartar, gingivitis, gum recession, and tooth loss. Being vigilant about dental care is the best way to save your dog's teeth.

Dental care begins in puppyhood, as you teach your Yorkie to enjoy getting his teeth brushed. You can use a soft-bristle toothbrush and meat-flavored doggy toothpaste. Because dogs don't spit, the foaming agents in human toothpaste can make them feel sick, and the high sodium content of baking powder is unhealthy. Make it a habit to brush once a day.

If you let plaque build up, it attracts bacteria and minerals, which harden into tartar. The plaque spreads rootward, causing irreversible periodontal disease with tissue, bone, and tooth loss. The bacteria gain an inlet to the bloodstream, where they can cause kidney and heart valve infections.

Although they won't take the place of brushing, hard, crunchy foods can help. Special foods are available from your veterinarian that are designed to scrape against the dog's teeth. They allow the tooth to penetrate deep inside the kibble before the kibble breaks, and have abrasive properties that scour the tooth surface. These foods may not be able to work miracles, but they are help-ful, especially for dogs who will not allow you to brush their teeth. If tartar accumulates, your Yorkshire may need a thorough cleaning under anesthesia.

Small Dog Nutrition

You have your choice of preparing a home-made diet for your dog or buying a commer-cial dog food. No matter which you choose, don't skimp because of price. A high-quality diet will be more than worth the extra pennies a day it costs to feed a tiny Yorkie in terms of increased health.

In order to choose a commercial food, you need to under-stand the information on the label.

Ingredient list. All ingredients in a food must be listed in order according to percentage weight, from highest to lowest. It's generally a good rule of thumb to look for foods in which the first several ingredients are mostly meat-based.

Guaranteed analysis. The guaranteed analysis chart represents the minimal percentages of crude protein and crude fat, and the maximum percentages of crude fiber and moisture, present in a food. The term "crude" means that the level is determined indirectly—for example, by measuring nitrogen to determine protein. The drawback to this index is that it doesn't measure protein quality or digestibility.

The fat percentage is handy in comparing the calories two kinds of food may contain, since fat has roughly double the calories of protein or carbohydrates. If fiber and moisture content are the same in two kinds of food, the higher-fat-content food will have more calories.

Crude fiber is an estimate of how much of the food is indigestible. Higher levels of crude fiber are often found in weight-reducing diets.

Calories. Dog food labels don't include calories, so you may need to calculate them yourself. Proteins and carbohydrates both have about 3.5 calories per gram, and fat has about 8.5 calories per gram. By multiplying 3.5 times the percentage of protein and carbohydrates listed in the analysis, and 8.5 times the percentage of fat, and then adding these products together, you will have the total number of calories per gram of a food.

Comparing Dry and Wet Dog Food

You'll notice that dry foods seem jam-packed with nutrition compared to wet foods. Wet foods have so much water in them that it makes their nutritive content look, well, watered down. To compare dry foods to wet foods, you have to factor out the differing moisture content so you compare them on their dry matter. Here's how:

1. Subtract the listed moisture content from each.
2. Take the remaining number you get (the food's dry matter) and divide it into each listed nutrient percentage.

So for a canned food with a listed moisture content of 80 percent and protein of 5 percent, you divide 5 by 20 to get 25. The canned food contains 25 percent protein on a dry matter basis.

Don't like doing even that much math? Here's a quick cheat. To compare the values in canned food with those in dry food, multiply the canned values by 4. If the canned food is "in gravy," multiply them by 5.

Home-Prepared Diets

You can also prepare your Yorkie's meals from scratch, mixing ingredients once a week or so and freezing them until needed. The meat can be cooked or raw, although the latter is controversial. No scientific data exist to prove that a raw diet is better, but many people who feed raw diets feel their dogs are healthier, with fewer skin and teeth problems, than when they were fed a commercial diet. Nonetheless, although dogs are more resistant to food

poisoning than people are, they're not immune, and they can also pass germs like salmonella along to humans they interact with. Many veterinary nutritionists advise that if you wish to feed a raw diet, you should only feed meat that is not ground, and you should first sear the outside of the meat to remove surface bacteria.

Many books are available with recipes for home-prepared diets. Never try to devise such a diet based on what you feel would be good. It's too easy to give too much or too little of certain nutrients, which can cause severe health problems. Make sure you only follow diets devised by veterinary nutritionists.

Supplements

There's no need to supplement most high-quality commercial foods, but many owners feel they must. If you supplement a commercial diet with meat, make sure it makes up no more than 10 percent of the total diet.

Vitamins. Most commercial diets contain enough vitamins and minerals that you won't need to add any. Nonetheless, many owners opt to add a dog vitamin to their pets' daily treats. Vitamins marketed for humans are made for human weight and contain too high a vitamin concentration for a small dog, unless only a fraction is given. Excessive amounts of most vitamins are simply excreted and do no harm, but excessive amounts of some, such as vitamins A and D, can be harmful. For example:

- Excess vitamin A has toxic effects on the liver, especially if the liver is already taxed because of other toxins or drugs.
- Excess vitamin D can lead to kidney damage and cause calcification of soft tissue. The same is true with minerals. Excessive amounts of most minerals won't harm a normal, healthy dog, but excessive levels can harm dogs with special needs. For instance:
- Excess copper can cause liver damage in dogs that cannot excrete copper normally.
- Excess phosphorus in dogs with kidney disease can cause problems similar to those caused by excessive vitamin D.
- Excess calcium is not appropriate for growing or pregnant dogs. Puppies under 6 months of age are especially susceptible to damage from excess calcium, which can lead to skeletal problems and osteochondrosis. Pregnant bitches given calcium supplements are more prone to develop eclampsia when nursing.

Other supplements may be helpful in some cases of illness.

Essential fatty acids (EFAs). EFAs are important in maintaining healthy skin and hair and in kidney function and reproduction. Linoleic acid is found in most vegetable oils and is popular among owners seeking to improve skin and fur quality, especially in cases of itching or disorders producing dry, flaky skin. Omega-3 fatty acids help reduce inflammation and may be helpful for dogs with arthritis, allergies, kidney disease, and heart disease. Omega-6 fatty acids may help synthesize the natural oils of the skin. A little goes a long way; too much of any fatty acid can cause diarrhea or even weight gain.

Breed Truths

Calorie Requirements

Typical maintenance daily calorie requirements for a 10-pound dog are as follows:

Active young adult	436 calories
Active adult	436 calories
Inactive adult	296 calories
Active senior	237 calories

Chondroitin sulfate and glucosamine. These popular supplements for dogs with arthritis work by affecting the cartilage matrix and synovial membrane. They have been shown to reduce some arthritic symptoms in humans, and studies in dogs show that a combination of the two reduces arthritic signs from cruciate disease.

Coenzyme Q10 (CoQ10). CoQ10 is an antioxidant and is required for energy production by cells. It's often used for patients with heart disease, allergies, periodontal disease, and, sometimes, cancer.

Zinc. Zinc has received a lot of attention in recent years because of its association with healthy skin. Dogs with inadequate levels of zinc in their diets often have hair loss and thickened and scabby skin. Some skin problems are actually termed "zinc-responsive," because they improve with zinc supplementation. Essential fatty acids can increase the body's ability to absorb zinc, whereas excessive calcium supplementation may reduce the absorption of zinc.

Brewer's yeast. Brewer's yeast has long been a popular supplement because of the widespread belief that it helps control fleas. Controlled studies have disputed this claim, but many owners still maintain that it works. Because it contains high levels of phosphorus, it shouldn't be used in young puppies or in dogs with kidney problems.

Many supplements may be helpful for dogs with health problems, but overall, most are probably unnecessary if you are feeding a high-quality commercial diet or a well-balanced home-prepared one.

Yorkshire Terrier Weight

Gauge how much to feed your Yorkie by how much he eats and how much he weighs. His coat may hide his figure somewhat, so you need to use your hands to determine if he's underweight or overweight. You should be able to feel the ribs slightly when you run your hands along the ribcage. An indication of a waistline should be visible both from above and from the side.

There should be no dimple in front of the tail, nor fat roll on the withers.

Some disorders, such as heart disease, Cushing's disease, hypothyroidism, and the early stages of diabetes, can cause a dog to appear fat or potbellied. A dog whose abdomen only is enlarged is especially suspect and should be examined by a veterinarian. A bloated belly in a puppy may signal internal parasites.

Most fat Yorkies are fat simply because they eat more calories than they burn. They need to lose weight, which you can achieve by feeding smaller portions of a lower-calorie food. Commercially available diet foods supply about 15 percent fewer calories compared to standard foods. Protein levels should remain moderate to high to avoid

FYI: Table Scraps

A few table scraps won't hurt, as long as they don't cut into your Yorkie's balanced diet. But choose your scraps carefully. Avoid hunks of fat, which can bring on pancreatitis in susceptible dogs, and avoid the following human foods that are toxic to dogs:

- **Chocolate** contains the stimulant theobromine, which can cause shaking, seizures, increased heart rate, and death in dogs. Milk chocolate has about 44 milligrams of theobromine per ounce, semisweet chocolate about 150 milligrams per ounce, and baker's chocolate about 390 milligrams per ounce. About 50 to 100 milligrams per pound is considered a lethal dose for dogs. One ounce of baker's chocolate could kill a 5-pound Yorkie.
- **Coffee** in large amounts, and especially coffee beans or grounds, can cause caffeine toxicity in dogs.
- **Sugar-free candy and gum** containing the artificial sweetener xylitol can cause a potentially fatal drop in blood sugar and lead to liver failure. A 5-pound Yorkie that eats as little as a quarter gram of xylitol needs veterinary treatment.
- **Onions** cause a condition in which the red blood cells are destroyed, in extreme cases leading to anemia and even death. Garlic contains the same ingredient, but in lesser quantity.

- **Macadamia nuts** cause some dogs to became very ill; the exact cause isn't understood.
- **Raisins and grapes** can cause kidney failure and extreme sudden toxicity in some dogs. As little as 0.3 ounces of grapes per pound, and 0.05 ounces of raisins per pound, have caused kidney failure in some dogs.
- **Yeast bread dough** can rise in the gastrointestinal tract, causing obstruction. It also produces alcohol as it rises.
- **Alcohol** can make dogs drunk just as it does people. It can also kill dogs if they drink too much, which could easily happen with a tiny dog.
- **Raw eggs**, contrary to popular opinion, are not good for dogs. They prevent the absorption of biotin, an important B vitamin. They can also contain salmonella.
- **Apple, apricot, cherry, peach and plum pits and stems** contain a cyanide-type compound. Signs of toxicity include dilated pupils, difficulty breathing, fast breathing, and shock.
- **Nutmeg** in large amounts can cause toxicity in dogs. Signs include tremors, seizures and even death.
- **Spoiled food** is no safer for dogs than it is for you. It can cause food poisoning, with signs including vomiting, diarrhea, and even death. Moldy food can cause nervous system signs such as tremors.

muscle loss when dieting. It's hard to resist those pleading eyes when your Yorkie begs for a treat, but treats add up to lots of calories during the day, especially in such a small dog. Substitute carrot sticks or rice cakes for fattening treats. Keep him away from where you prepare and eat human meals, and instead of feeding him leftovers when you're through eating, make it a habit to go for a walk.

BE PREPARED! Small Dog Nutrition

Some dog food companies market foods specifically designed for the needs of small dogs. Whether you feed your Yorkie one of these foods or not, keep these factors in mind:

- Small dogs must eat more per pound than big dogs. According to one study, a 6-pound Yorkie must eat about 47 calories per pound of body weight in order to maintain weight and condition. In contrast, a 100-pound dog only needs 23 calories per pound of body weight.

- Small dogs have small stomachs. That means you can't just feed your Yorkie a lot of food to make sure he gets enough calories. You may need to feed him more calorie-rich food and more small meals per day.

- Small dogs don't eat a lot of food overall, so small snacks can throw off the balance of his diet.

- Small dogs, especially very small or very young ones, must eat a little, often, in order to ward off hypoglycemia.

- Small dogs should eat foods rich in complex carbohydrates, and avoid simple sugars, in order to ward off hypoglycemia.

- Small dogs need small kibble so they can crunch it up rather than have to swallow it whole. Optimally kibble designed doesn't simply break up when chewed, but requires the tooth to penetrate it before breaking, adding to its scrubbing action.

- Small dogs tend to have dental problems, and if their teeth are in bad shape they may not be able to eat hard food at all, or may require a softer kibble.

- Small dogs lose more body heat in cold weather compared to large dogs. The Yorkie's coat, although long, lacks an undercoat. In fact, the hair density is about half that of other breeds. Because his coat provides little insulation against the cold, the Yorkie's food should have ample fat content to make up for energy lost in maintaining body heat.

- Small dogs tend to be somewhat discriminating in their tastes, even picky. This may be because they have a small olfactory area compared to other dogs and may not be able to smell and appreciate foods as much as larger breeds. It may also be because they live more closely with their owners than do many large dogs, and are used to tasting tidbits from their owners' plates. Different breeds do tend to have different appetites, and Yorkies are not among the breeds known to vacuum their food bowl no matter what is in it.

- In order to grow a healthy coat, Yorkies need good nutrition. Good hair growth requires high-quality protein, essential fatty acids, vitamin B complex, vitamin C, vitamin E, and minerals such as zinc, among others (see page 142).

Underweight dogs. It's not unusual for adolescents to be a little on the lean side, but a thin puppy or adult, or an adolescent whose backbone and hipbones can be seen, should be checked by your veterinarian. Weight loss or failure to gain weight could be caused by a liver shunt, heart disease, cancer, or any number of endocrine problems. If he checks out normal, you may be able to add pounds by feeding more meals of a higher-calorie food. Add canned food, ground beef, or a small amount of chicken fat. Heating the food will often increase its appeal. You can also add a late-night snack; many dogs seem to have their best appetites late at night.

10 **Questions** About Liver Shunts

1 I heard that a lot of Yorkies have something called a liver shunt. What is that?
When a dog is still in the womb, his dam's liver does the job of filtering out toxins, storing sugar, and producing protein for the fetus. Because the fetus's liver doesn't have to do anything, a large blood vessel carries blood quickly through or around it. This blood vessel normally closes up around birth, when the puppy's own liver takes over. But sometimes the blood vessel stays open, diverting much of the blood from the liver so the blood doesn't get processed as it should. This is called a liver, or portosystemic, shunt, because it shunts the blood away from the liver. The shunt can be either inside (intrahepatic) or outside (extrahepatic) the liver.

2 Do liver shunts cause health problems? A Yorkie with a liver shunt might be unusually small, with poor muscular development because of the lack of protein. He might also have behavioral abnormalities, such as seizures, circling, unresponsiveness, head pressing, or just staring into space or acting unusually quiet for a puppy. These signs are most common a few hours after a large meal, especially a high-protein meal. Less commonly, the dog may vomit, have diarrhea, or drink and urinate too much. Some puppies have no apparent signs, and liver shunt may not be suspected until they take an abnormally long time recovering from anesthesia or sedatives. Most often, signs are noticed within the first two years of life.

3 How common are liver shunts in Yorkies? Yorkies are thirty-six times more likely to have a liver shunt than all other breeds combined. Like other small breeds, Yorkies are more likely to have the extrahepatic type of shunt, where the shunt forms outside of the liver. Although the exact mode of inheritance is unknown, liver shunts are considered to be hereditary in Yorkshire Terriers. One study found them to be more common in highly inbred Yorkies than in less inbred Yorkies. Affected dogs should not be bred. If your dog is affected, you should notify his breeder.

4 How are liver shunts diagnosed? A first test is usually a blood sample. A Yorkie with a liver shunt may be slightly anemic or have increases in liver enzymes. A urine sample may be unusually dilute or contain abnormal crystals. These abnormal results can be caused by many other problems, so if present, your veterinarian will want to perform more specialized tests.

A bile acid test checks for abnormally high levels of bile acids in the blood, which are indicative of liver disease. Two blood samples are usually taken. About 95 percent of Yorkies with liver shunts will have elevated bile acids.

Scintigraphy is a more advanced test that measures blood flow through the liver. If an abnormally high percentage ends up in the heart, it means the dog has a liver shunt.

A portogram provides an X-ray of the blood vessels to the liver. Unlike scintigraphy, it can tell whether a shunt is inside or outside the liver, and can give the veterinarian a picture of where it is located and if there is more than one.

How do I care for a dog with a liver shunt? Diet can help manage some problems by reducing the toxins produced by protein. Special diets are available that have low levels of high-quality protein derived from dairy or vegetable sources. Do not feed a dog with liver shunts red meat or fish! Whereas most commercial foods for adult dogs contain about 25 percent protein on a dry matter basis, and higher for puppies, you want to feed a diet with no more than 18 percent protein on a dry matter basis. The food should also be low in copper and iron, and contain vitamins and antioxidants.

 What about surgery? Surgery is the best hope for dogs with liver shunts. It is more successful if performed by an experienced veterinarian, particularly a board-certified veterinary surgeon. These professionals can be found at veterinary teaching hospitals or referral centers.

How long will it take to recover from surgery? It will take the dog a few days to recover from the surgery, and he will still need to stay on a low-protein diet for a couple of months. Additional blood tests and a scintigraphy can be performed to make sure the shunt is closed. About 85 percent of dogs treated with ameroid constrictor surgery go on to live normal lives; about 15 percent must continue to be managed with special diet and medicine for life.

 How can I avoid getting a Yorkie with a liver shunt? Choose an adult and have him tested with a blood test or a bile acid test—before you bring him home. When buying a puppy, ask about liver shunts or screening tests in the parents or relatives of the puppy. Avoid puppies from breeders who never test for shunts or don't know what you're talking about. Look for puppies from litters that are not inbred. Wait until the puppies are 18 weeks of age, when they can have bile acid tests run.

 How can this problem be eradicated from the breed? Scientists continue to search for better ways to predict, prevent, diagnose, and treat liver shunts. Researchers at Cornell University are working to develop a DNA test that could detect if both parents share genes for the disorder.

 Where can I find more information?
- American College of Veterinary Surgeons
  This site also allows you to search for a surgeon in your area.
  www.acvs.org/AnimalOwners/ HealthConditions/SmallAnimalTopics/ PortosystemicShunts(PSS)
- Purina Update
  Excellent review.
  http://yorkiefoundation.org/purina1.pdf
- University of Tennessee
  (Dr. Tobias at UT is at the forefront of liver shunt research and treatment.)
  www.vet.utk.edu/clinical/sacs/shunt/faq.php

103

Chapter Seven

Training and Activities

Yorkies are fine lapdogs, but don't get too comfortable. They like to do things, all sorts of things, to the point where you may feel like an activities director. The first step in any sort of activity, though, is having a well-trained Yorkie you can take places with a reasonable expectation that he will behave himself.

Many Yorkie owners see no need to train such a little dog, but all dogs benefit from training. You'd like him to walk on a leash without tripping you, greet people without mauling them, and be quiet when in public. Yorkies have the advantage of being able to go with you to many places big dogs can't, as long as they are carried in a pet bag. Even then, they need to behave.

Train Positively!

Forget what you learned about dog training a decade or so ago. Modern training methods focus on rewards and positive associations rather than force and punishment. They produce happy, well-trained dogs that are eager to learn more. Most training classes now encourage the use of treats and toys as motivators and rewards. Praise is still important, but for most dogs, the way to their brains is through their stomachs. Like you, they like to be paid for a job well done, and they're not above being materialistic.

That doesn't mean you're sentenced to a life as a walking treat dispenser. When you first teach your Yorkie something, you'll want to reward him every time he does it right. But once he knows it, you can cut back gradually, rewarding him only some of the times, but still praising every time. Just like a gambler at the slot machines, most dogs will work with the expectation that the next time might bring the treat jackpot. Again, only give treats sometimes, but give praise all the time.

If you train your dog before his regular meal time he'll work much better for food. In fact, instead of giving treats in addition to your dog's regular food, you can dole out his dinner bit by bit as rewards during training sessions. If you're in a hurry, just train for a few minutes, give a few rewards, and then give a jackpot of his entire meal.

Clicker Training

Many progressive obedience instructors use clicker training, which is a type of training used by professional animal trainers. A click is merely a signal that you use to help tell your dog when he's doing something right. It's a distinctive noise that takes the place of saying "Good!" to mark the instant when your dog is doing what you want. It works better than the word "Good!" because your dog notices an unusual sound (in this case, a click) more than he notices your words. You can buy a clicker at a pet supply store, or use anything that makes a distinctive sound.

Breed Needs

Training Equipment

Because the training methods described here don't rely on force, you won't need to use a choke collar for training. A buckle collar, or even a harness, will suffice. You will also want a 6-foot leash (not chain!) and maybe a 20-foot light line. And you'll need lots of tiny treats that he can gobble down quickly.

By following the click sound with a reward, your dog quickly learns that the click means "Yes, that's it!" Because the click is faster and shorter than your voice, it can more precisely mark the moment your dog is doing something right.

The click also tells the dog he can end the behavior, so once you click, don't expect him to continue sitting or doing whatever you've been teaching him. Once he understands how to do something, you can phase out the click, but not the praise and rewards.

To start clicker training, you'll want lots of tiny treats. You can start by simply clicking and then giving your dog a treat, so he learns that a click means a treat is coming. You'll need to do this at least

FYI: Training Tips

- Teach new behaviors in a quiet place away from distractions. Only when your dog knows the behavior very well should you gradually start practicing it in other places.
- Although you can train your Yorkie off leash when you are in a safe, enclosed area, train him on a leash when you are in an unfenced area.
- Don't train your dog when he's hot, tired, or has just eaten. You want him peppy and alert for class time!
- Don't train your dog if you're impatient or mad. You won't be able to hide your frustration, and your dog will be uneasy.
- No dog learns to do something perfectly at first. Always train in gradual steps. Give rewards for getting closer and closer to the final behavior. Be patient!
- Give your dog feedback ("Good!") instantly when he does what you want. The faster you mark the behavior like this, the easier it is for your dog to figure out what you like. Think of it as taking a picture of the moment you want to show to the dog and say "Do this again!"
- Give a reward as soon as you can after saying "Good!"
- Don't forget to praise your dog as part of the reward!

- Don't start using a cue word ("Sit," "Down," and the like) until your dog knows the behavior.
- Just say a cue word once. Repeating it over and over won't help your dog learn it.
- Dogs learn better in short sessions. Train your Yorkie for only about 10 to 15 minutes at a time. Always quit while he's still having fun. You can train him several times a day if you want.
- Try to end your training sessions doing something your dog can do well. You want to end on a high note!
- Don't push your Yorkie too fast. His successes should far outweigh his failures. Just like you, dogs like to do things they're good at.
- Every step has to be repeated many, many times—we're talking hundreds of times to get it right sometimes! Be patient!
- If your Yorkie has a hard time learning one particular thing, skip it and try a different behavior or a different way of teaching it. If he's smart enough to figure out how to find his food bowl, he's smart enough to learn a behavior. You just have to figure out how to talk to him in his language and make it worth his while.

20 times before he'll start to look at your treat hand expectantly after he hears the click. Once you start training, remember:

- Give a click instantly when your dog does what you want. The faster you click, the easier it is for him to figure out what you like.
- Give a reward as soon as you can after the click.

In this chapter, anywhere it says to use the word "Good!" you can substitute your clicker sound.

Obedience Classes

Dog obedience classes train you to train your dog. Don't expect to drop your dog off and have somebody else do all the work. You'll get more out of it by learning how your Yorkie learns. Most of your learning takes place at class, whereas most of your dog's learning takes place at your home practice sessions.

Puppy Kindergarten

Dogs that are exposed to the concepts of learning at a young age are much more adept at learning new things when adults. Puppy kindergarten allows puppies to learn to learn, and to socialize with other dogs and people in a structured setting. Classes help your dog learn to enjoy going places with you, and help him become a well-behaved member of public gatherings that include other dogs. They provide a setting in which to teach new skills or cope with budding behavior problems under the supervision of an experienced instructor.

Kindergarten classes are generally open to dogs between the ages of 12 weeks and 6 months, although a small Yorkie might be better off waiting a little longer before starting or graduating. Your veterinarian can advise you if your puppy's inoculations are sufficient to begin class. The class should require proof of inoculations from participants, and you should ask if any puppies with contagious diseases have been in the class recently.

Look for classes that emphasize reward-based training using play, toys, and treats. Avoid classes that advocate physical punishment, chain choke collars, neck scruffing, shaking, or alpha rolls (in which you force the puppy on his back and hold him there until he submits).

Play is an equal part of learning, and kindergarten classes often let your puppy practice fetching and other simple games and tricks. You don't have to participate in every exercise, so if you think something is not appropriate for your puppy, take a break and let your dog have a rest. Most kindergarten classes have a play time for the puppies, but that's not a time for them to run amuck and be bullied or pick on each other. If that happens, you need to find a more appropriate playmate, or remove your dog. Neither bullying nor being picked on is a good experience for him or the other puppy, and a good instructor should prevent it from happening.

Puppy kindergarten can give your Yorkie puppy a great foundation for the future—but it's just a foundation. It doesn't take the place of adult

Helpful Hints

Finding a Class Act

Ask your breeder, local veterinarian, groomer, pet supply store, or rescue group for suggestions about classes. You can also contact local kennel clubs or obedience clubs (find them through www.akc.org), which may offer classes. Or go to the Web site of the Association of Pet Dog Trainers (www.apdt.org) to see if any are listed near you.

classes; it simply helps make them easier. Nor does attending class once a week provide enough training. Classes are where you learn to train your dog and where you show off what he's learned in a distracting setting. The real training takes place at home, by you, in a quiet setting where the two of you won't be distracted.

Adult Classes

If your Yorkie has graduated from kindergarten, he'll probably be disappointed he has no place to go see friends and have fun anymore. Don't worry; most towns also have adult obedience classes. Evaluate these classes the same way you would puppy classes. You may be able to choose from beginner, basic, and advanced curricula. Such classes are great places to keep your Yorkie in practice, learn even more, and socialize with other people who share an interest in their dogs. If you plan to compete in obedience, go into therapy work, or do anything that involves your dog in public, going to class will keep him in practice.

The Basic Exercises

Your Yorkie is capable of learning all sorts of things, from circus tricks to how to trick you into just about anything. But even if you don't have aspirations to amaze your friends with your dog's incredible mind, you need to teach him basic obedience exercises, which are walking on leash, sitting, lying down, coming when called, and staying on command.

Leash Walking

Leash training is often a pup's first introduction to formal training. In the old days, trainers often advocated dragging the dog until he tired of fighting the leash, but there's no need for that. Here's what you do:

1. Place a buckle collar on the puppy and attach a leash. You may need to use a cat collar and leash.
2. Lure him forward with a treat and give it to him. Keep luring him forward a little more and more as you walk slowly along with him at your side. Give him the treat every few steps.
3. If he wants to go in a different direction, or stops and bucks, go ahead and walk in his direction a few steps before trying to lure him along again. If he absolutely refuses to move, carry him a short distance away and see if he'll walk back with you to some place he wants to go.
4. As he gets better, you can ignore him when he balks, being sure to reward as soon as he lets the leash get slack.
5. If he pulls ahead on the leash, dragging you, stop dead in your tracks. Don't pull back; just stand there. Only when he lets the leash go slack do you say "Good!" and reward or move forward. Practice this until he stops pulling as soon as you stop.
6. Next, walk toward something he wants to reach. If he pulls, stop or even back up. The point is not to jerk your dog back, but to show him that pulling gets him there more slowly. When he stops pulling, go toward the goal again. The goal is his reward, but the only way he can reach it is to stop pulling!

Heel

Most of the time you'll be content that your dog walks on a leash without pulling or lunging, but there are times when you'd like him to stay right at your side in *heel* position. *Heel* position is on your left side, with your dog's neck level with your leg.

It's difficult to guide a small dog to the proper place at your side because the length of the leash still allows him a lot of leeway. You can cope with this in several ways. First, you can rely upon luring your dog into position using treats. One way to do this is with a long stick with some gooey treat, such as squeeze cheese or liverwurst, stuck to the end. You then simply move the stick until he's in position, then tell him "Good!" and let him lick the treat off. If you prefer to guide with a leash, you can string your leash through a hollow piece of PVC that extends almost to the dog, so that the pivot point is just a few inches higher than the dog.

Here's how to teach your dog to *heel* in position:

1. Maneuver your dog into *heel* position using either the leash or the treat on a stick. Once he is there, say "Good!" and reward him.
2. As he starts to get in position reliably, add the cue "Heel!" Be sure to reward him.
3. Practice without the guidance of the solid leash or treat.
4. After he is heeling while you walk calmly, make staying in *heel* position a game by running and turning, and rewarding him when he is able to stick by your side.

Sit

Sitting is one of the easier skills you can teach your dog, and one of the handiest as well. If you teach it as one of your puppy's first tricks, he'll use it as his favored trick when he wants something, and be inclined to *sit* as though to say "please."

You can teach a dog to *sit* in many ways, but one of the easiest is to lure him into sitting, as follows:

1. Hold a treat just above and behind the level of his eyes. If he bends his knees and points his nose up, mark the behavior and reward him. If instead he walks backward, you can practice with his rear end a few inches from a corner to prevent him from backing up.
2. Repeat this several times, each time moving the lure further back, until finally your dog is sitting reliably upon your command. Yorkies don't have far to go!
3. Next, repeat using only your hand without a treat to guide him. When he sits, give him a treat from your other hand.
4. Gradually abbreviate your hand movements until you are only using a small hand signal.
5. When he is sitting reliably, add the verbal cue "Sit!" right before the hand signal. The verbal signal will come to predict the hand signal, and he will soon learn to *sit* to either.

Down

Having a Yorkie who will lie down quietly is helpful both for good manners and for safety, as it can keep him out from underfoot. To teach your Yorkie to lie down on command:

1. Place him on a raised surface and have him sit.
2. Show him a treat and move it forward and downward.
3. If his elbows touch the ground, say "Good!" and reward him. Even if he only goes partway, reward him. Then repeat, rewarding him for going down further. If he keeps trying to get up, you can place your hands over his shoulders to gently help guide him downward.

4. Next, repeat without a treat in the hand you have been using to lure him. When he sits, give him a treat from your other hand.

5. Gradually abbreviate your hand movements until you are only using a small hand signal.

6. Add the verbal cue "Down" right before the hand signal.

7. Practice the *down-stay* just as you did the *sit-stay*.

8. Then teach him the *down* command from a standing position.

Stay

Sitting and staying aren't very useful if your dog just hops right up. He needs a separate command that tells him to stay in position until you tell him he can move. Because staying is essentially asking the dog to do nothing, it's taught by introducing the cue word ("Stay") right from the start. Otherwise he won't know the difference between a *sit* or *down* where you forgot to reward him and this new behavior of not moving. Here's how to teach your Yorkie to stay:

1. Cue your dog to sit. Say "Stay" and hold your palm in a "stop" signal in front of his face. Wait for a few seconds, then reward him and say "OK!"

ACTIVITIES Fetch!

The best time to teach your puppy to fetch is as soon as possible. The longer you wait, the greater the chance your Yorkie will simply look at you quizzically when you throw something, as if to ask why you don't go get it yourself.

The best place to teach your puppy to fetch is in a hallway. Otherwise, you can use a long, lightweight line to prevent the dog from running off with the prize. You want him to learn that he gets rewarded for bringing it back to you. Don't steal the prize from him; trade it for a treat and then give it back or throw it again.

Try tossing the toy so it scoots along the floor, or if you have a small ball, bounce it against the wall. Different dogs are excited by different types of toys and movements. Try a feathery cat toy tied to a leash or string, and jiggle and jerk it enticingly around the dog, ending with a toss. Or use a plush puppy toy or a ball and toss it. Make sure to use a special toy the dog doesn't get to play with otherwise. Always stop when the dog still wants to play more.

Once he's got the "chase and grab" part down, then work on the "bring it back" part. If he knows how to come when called, you can call him, but he may drop the toy first. Or you can run away from him, which will usually have him running to you. If he won't bring it, try giving him less room until he has no choice but to bring it to you, then rewarding him and throwing it again. If you position yourself in the middle of a long hall, you can take one toy and immediately throw another to the opposite end of the hall, a game many puppies relish.

A dog who enjoys fetching is a dog who will enjoy playing with you for years to come. He can be entertained and exercise indoors, and can even be taught to pick small things up from the ground for you. Don't put it off!

2. Tell him "Stay" and give him the stop signal, then pivot out in front of him. If your dog is having a problem getting the concept, you can have him sit on a raised surface or behind a small barrier so it's more difficult for him to move. Always be sure to reward him before you give him the "OK" signal.
3. Work up gradually to a longer duration. If he gets up, simply put him back in position and start over, decreasing the duration you expect of him.
4. Next, work on moving to different positions around your dog, still remaining close to him. Move in front, to either side, and behind your dog, and gradually move farther away.
5. Introduce mild distractions, gradually working up to greater ones. Remember, you want your dog to succeed!
6. Now you are ready to work on the *stay* in other locations. Be sure to keep him on lead for his safety when practicing in public areas. Eventually your dog should be steady just about anywhere.
7. Do the same thing with the *down* position.

Come

Your Yorkie probably already comes to you when he wants to interact. Always make sure you reward him for coming, even when you haven't called him. Your real goal, however, is to have him come when called. The best time to start is when your dog is still a puppy, when he's less independent. Here's one way to teach a reliable *come* on command:

1. You will need a friend to help you, and a long hallway or other enclosed area. Have your helper hold your dog while you back away, showing your dog a treat or toy.
2. Once your dog obviously wants to go to you, your helper should release him so he can run to you. You can even turn and run away to increase your puppy's enthusiasm. Say "Good!" the moment he reaches you, then quickly reward him.
3. Eventually you want to be able to touch his collar so you don't end up with a dog that dances around just outside your reach. To do that, wait until you touch or hold his collar before rewarding him.
4. Once he is running to you reliably, add the cue "Come!" just before your helper releases him. Practice this several times for many sessions.
5. Once he is coming on cue, let him meander around on his own. Call "Come" and reward him when he lets you touch his collar.
6. Finally, practice in lots of different places, gradually choosing places with more distractions. Keep your dog on a long light line for his safety.

Always make coming to you rewarding. If you want your dog to come so you can give him a bath or put him to bed or do anything else he doesn't really like, go get him rather than call him. Practice calling him when outdoors or even around the house, giving him a reward, and then leaving him on his own again.

Teach Your Yorkie to Watch You

Every instructor knows that the first challenge in teaching is getting your pupil's attention. A dog that pays attention on command has a huge advantage when it comes to minding you in public places. Here's how you can teach him to do that.

1. When your dog looks at your face, say "Good!" and reward him.
2. Soon he'll figure out that looking at your face gets him a reward, and he'll do it more often. Repeat this until he's looking at your face reliably.
3. Now add a distraction by holding the treat away from you, to the side. Your dog will look at it and perhaps try to get it, but don't let him. Only when he glances back at your face should you say "Good!" and reward him.
4. Work up gradually until he has to look at you for five seconds, even with the treat held to the side.
5. When he's doing that reliably, add the cue "Watch me!" just as he begins to turn toward you. Repeat that, then start rewarding him only

when he looks to you after you have said "Watch me!" You should still praise and pet him for looking at you without being cued; paying attention to you is always a good thing!

6. Once he is reliably watching you on cue, put him in more distracting situations and practice there. Start with minimal distractions and graduate to more distracting locales only when he is paying attention on cue. It may take a long time to get his attention in each new place, but be patient.

Tricks

Yorkies are natural showoffs, and many take to tricks naturally. Start with some of the classics, then make up your own using the same concept of gradually shaping the behavior until he gets it right. Be sure to make it fun!

Shake Hands

1. Kneel facing him as he is sitting. If you want, have him sit on an elevated surface.
2. Reach for his right paw with your right hand. He may naturally give you his paw, but if he doesn't, use a treat to lure his head way to the left, so he's almost looking over his shoulder. That will make his right paw lift. Praise and reward him as soon as his paw goes up.

3. Keep repeating, until he starts lifting his paw on his own.
4. Add the cue word "Shake hands," and only give him your hand and reward him when he shakes on cue.

Roll Over

1. Start with him lying down. Show him a treat and move it over his back so he has to twist his head over his shoulder to see it. Give him the treat, and next time have him twist a little more before he gets it. Keep on asking for more and more, until he eventually ends up rolling over. You can help a bit at this point with a gentle nudge.
2. Once he's on his back, keep moving the treat to the opposite side so he has to finish the roll and end up back on his stomach before getting the treat.
3. Once he can do a complete roll easily, add the cue "Roll over!" Only reward him for rolling over on cue. You can keep on adding roll after roll. Just don't get him too dizzy to do the next trick!

Speak

Teaching your Yorkie to speak on cue is not only a fun trick but a way to teach him the difference between desirable barking and undesirable barking.

1. First, figure out what makes him bark. The best situation is if he barks at you to urge you to give him a treat. Once he barks, say "Good!" and reward him.
2. Introduce the cue word ("Speak!") quickly for this trick. You don't want to reward him for speaking out of turn!
3. Once you've introduced the cue word, never reward him for speaking on his own.
4. While he is barking, introduce the cue word "Shhhhh." Reward him for stopping. Practice starting and stopping your dog from barking. This will help you stop him from barking when he's doing it on his own.

Canine Good Citizen

Yorkie owners like to take their dogs out on the town, visiting cafés and stores where dogs are allowed. This means it's especially important that your dog behave in public. If he barks and snaps, or throws himself on everyone he meets, he will give the breed a bad reputation, and just as important, the two of you will miss out on a lot of opportunities you could have shared because you had to leave him at home.

The American Kennel Club has outlined a series of exercises any dog should master to be a good public citizen. The AKC also offers a simple test whereby your dog can demonstrate his proficiency and earn the Canine Good Citizen (CGC) title. The test is done on leash; a long line is provided for the Stay and Recall exercises. The CGC title is one of the most important

CHECKLIST

Canine Good Citizen Exercises

✔ Accept a friendly stranger without acting shy or resentful, or breaking position to approach; sit politely for petting and allow the stranger to examine his ears, feet, and coat, and to brush him.

✔ Walk politely on a loose leash, turning and stopping with you, walking through a group of at least three other people without jumping on them, pulling, or acting overly exuberant, shy, or resentful. He need not be perfectly aligned with you, but he shouldn't be pulling.

✔ Sit and lie down on command (you can gently guide him into position) and then stay as you walk 20 feet away and back.

✔ Stay and then come to you when called from 10 feet away.

✔ Behave politely to another dog-and-handler team, showing only casual interest in them.

✔ React calmly to distractions such as a dropped chair or passing jogger without panicking, barking, or acting aggressively.

✔ Remain calm when held by a stranger while you're out of sight for 3 minutes.

✔ Refrain from eliminating, growling, snapping, biting, or attempting to attack a person or dog throughout the evaluation.

honors your Yorkie can earn. To find an upcoming CGC test, or to learn more about it, go to *www.akc.org/events/cgc/*.

Therapy Work

Dogs didn't earn the title of man's best friend just because they hunt and herd. They earned it because they really are best friends. They are true companions that many people find it easier to open up to than they do with other people. This is one reason that dogs are so successful in raising the spirits and encouraging interaction with people in a variety of situations. Yorkies excel at being best buddies, and many Yorkies visit people in nursing homes, children in hospitals, and homebound neighbors, who relish the chance to interact with a dog. They even visit schools because it's been found that reading to dogs helps children build confidence as readers.

Therapy dog training entails extensive socialization to people, places, and situations. Therapy dogs that visit hospitals or nursing homes must be comfortable around wheelchairs, walkers, and medical equipment. All therapy dogs must have basic obedience skills and be able to perform their jobs

Breed Truths

Service Dogs

When service dogs come to mind, most people think of guide dogs, which really is not a job suited for Yorkies! But Yorkies can work as service dogs. They can help disabled people by retrieving dropped items and generally acting as an agile set of extra hands that can reach the floor. Those trained as hearing dogs can alert hearing-impaired people to certain sounds. Seizure alert dogs alert their owners to impending seizures, and may also seek help. Psychiatric support dogs provide emotional support for owners with panic attacks or other disabling psychological problems. Many of these jobs require special training or certification. Service dogs require about two years of training, and even then, many don't work out. Training them to do the tasks is the easy part; training them to be reliable under any circumstance is the hard part. For more information, visit the Web sites of these service dog organizations:

Assistance Dogs International
www.adionline.org

Dogs for the Deaf, Inc.
www.dogsforthedeaf.org

International Association of Assistance Dog Partners
www.iaadp.org

Love on a Leash
www.loveonaleash.org

amidst many distractions. They should naturally love meeting new people in new places. It's not a job for an introvert; in fact, such a dog could hurt the feelings of a patient who might conclude he or she had done something wrong. However, some dogs do better with children, and some with seniors. Some like noisy situations, others like quiet ones. Some like to snuggle, others like to perform. Finding a particular dog's talents is an important part of preparation.

Therapy dogs must pass a test that includes obedience; the ability to leave food, toys, and medications alone when working; the ability to tolerate being petted all over; and the ability to be quiet when asked. Maybe the worst part of therapy dog preparation is learning to tolerate a bath before visits! Not only is it nicer to snuggle with a clean dog, but many therapy dogs visit people with fragile immune systems. Finally, therapy dog owners must know what to do in unexpected situations. They must protect their Yorkies from being hugged too hard, dropped, grabbed, or allowed to jump off a lap onto a slippery floor.

Most therapy dog certification requires the dog to first pass the Canine Good Citizen test (see previous section). He must then fulfill additional requirements, such as being around wheelchairs and walkers without getting upset; leaving food alone; remaining confident around people who shuffle, cough, or even shout; remaining calm when left alone with a trusted person; and being willing to greet a stranger. Dogs must be at least 1 year old. Several certifying organizations exist, but the two largest in North America are Therapy Dogs International (*www.tdi-dog.org*) and the Delta Society (*www.deltasociety.org*).

Competitions

Most Yorkie owners are perfectly content just knowing they have the best dog in the world. Some, however, enjoy proving it by earning titles and competing in various events. No matter what your dog's skills, there's a competition to show them off.

Rally

If your Yorkie enjoys learning obedience, a good place to prove his mettle is at a rally obedience event, in which you and your dog go through a course consisting of 10 to 20 signs, each of which has instructions telling you which exercise to perform. Some of these exercises are moving exercises, such as heeling at various paces, turning, circling, stepping to one side, or calling your dog to you. Others are stationary exercises, such as having your dog lie down, stay, or pivot in heel position. You can talk to your dog throughout and repeat commands, but you can't pull him along on his leash or touch him. Points are deducted for mistakes, but a lot of leeway is allowed. The emphasis is on teamwork rather than precision. Each course is different, and you won't get to see it until you arrive at the trial. That means you'll need to know all the possible exercises, even though you'll only be asked to do a subset of them. The novice exercises are fairly simple, consisting of heeling, coming, sitting, and lying down.

More advanced classes include low jumps; 90- and 180-degree pivots to either direction in which the dog stays in *heel* position at your side as you

FYI: Rally Classes and Titles

To earn a title, a dog must qualify three times at that level. The most advanced title, Rally Advanced Excellent (RAE) rally, is awarded to dogs who qualify ten times in both the Advanced class and the Excellent class at the same trial. Rally is a great way to get involved in obedience sports because it's fairly low key and a lot of fun!

Class	Title	Leash	# of signs	Stationary exercises	Jumps	Exercises
Novice	RN	on	10–15	no more than 5	0	basic list
Advanced	RA	off	12–17	no more than 7	1	novice plus pivots, call front, stand
Excellent	RE	off	15–20	no more than 7	1–2	advanced plus reverse, moving stand, honor

pivot; the dog starting and finishing in a sit; and an honor exercise, in which the dog remains in a *sit* or *down* position at the edge of the ring while another dog goes through the course. The honoring (staying) dog is on leash.

Each exercise has a particular sign with symbols that describe it, and each exercise has a particular way it should be performed. To find out more and see the signs, go to *www.rallyobedience.com*.

Obedience

Traditional obedience competitions require a little more precision than rally obedience. In these trials you can't talk or gesture to your dog except to give commands, and you can only praise between exercises. Instead of following printed directions, a judge tells you what to do as you go along. You get few, if any, second chances, and precision counts. Points are deducted for imperfections. High in Trial (HIT) is awarded to the top scorer of the day at an obedience trial.

Fun Facts

Rally First
The first Yorkie to earn the RAE title was CH, U-CD Caraleigh Terra-Billie Fair, CDX, RAE, RL2. Several have since followed.

Regular classes are Novice, Open, and Utility, but intermediate classes are also offered. Pre-Novice classes, for example, involve the same basic exercises as Novice but all on leash. To earn a title, your dog must pass every exercise in the class, and score a minimum number of available points. The standard titles, from entry level to advanced, are Companion Dog and Companion Dog Excellent. The Utility Dog Excellent title is awarded for qualifying in both Open and Utility classes on the same day at ten trials.

CHECKLIST

Novice Rally Exercises

- ✔ Halt and sit
- ✔ Halt and down
- ✔ 90-degree right and left turns
- ✔ 270-degree right and left turns
- ✔ Right and left about turns
- ✔ U-turn
- ✔ Right and left circles
- ✔ Call front from heel, then finish back to heel position from right or left
- ✔ Heel at normal, slow, and fast paces
- ✔ Moving sidestep to right
- ✔ Spiral with dog to inside and outside
- ✔ Weave around four pylons one or both ways

- ✔ Halt, take one step forward and halt (dog sits), two steps forward and halt, three steps forward and halt
- ✔ Call to front (dog sits), take one step backward and call dog to front again, two steps calling dog to front, three steps calling dog to front
- ✔ Lie down while heeling
- ✔ Fast forward from sit
- ✔ Walk around dog in *sit-stay* position and *down-stay* position

The Obedience Trial Champion (OTCH) is the supreme obedience title, requiring a dog to earn 100 points, plus three first placements by scoring better than other qualifying dogs in Open or Utility.

Agility

Agility is the sport for canine adrenaline addicts. It's an obstacle course for dogs run against the clock, combining jumping, climbing, weaving, running, zipping through tunnels, and loads of fun!

Several organizations, including the AKC, the United Kennel Club (UKC), the North American Dog Agility Council (NADAC), and the United States Dog Agility Association (USDAA) sponsor trials and award titles. The AKC program is described here, but don't discount the others, which many competitors find to be even more fun.

AKC agility is divided into two types of courses. The Standard course includes all the obstacle types, including those referred to as contact obstacles: the A-frame, Dog Walk, Teeter, and Pause Table. The Jumpers With Weaves (JWW) course includes only jumps, tunnels, and weaves, usually in a somewhat more intricate course pattern than the standard. Of course, not all dogs jump the same heights. Yorkies compete in either the 8-inch jump height division, for dogs 10 inches and under at the withers (top of shoulders), or in the 12-inch division, for dogs 10 to 14 inches at the withers. If this seems too high for your dog, you can enter the preferred classes, in which the jump heights in each division are 4 inches lower. Titles earned in these classes are the same as regular titles but end in a "P."

ACTIVITIES Obedience Exercises

Novice Exercises (three passes earn the Companion Dog (CD) title)
- Heeling on and off leash, with the dog sitting automatically each time you stop; negotiating right, left, and about turns, and changing to a faster and slower pace.
- Heeling on leash in a figure eight around two people.
- Standing off lead without moving while the judge touches him.
- Waiting for you to call and then coming from about 20 feet (about 6 m) away, and then returning to *heel* position on command.
- Staying in a *sit* position for one minute, and then a *down* position for three minutes, in a group of other dogs while you are 20 feet (about 6 m) away.

Open Exercises (three passes earns the Companion Dog Excellent (CDX) title)
- Heeling, including a figure-eight, off leash.
- Coming when called as in Novice, except dropping to a *down* position when told to do so about halfway back to you, and then continuing the recall when commanded.
- Retrieving a thrown dumbbell first over flat ground and then over a small jump.
- Jumping over a broad jump.
- Staying in a *sit* position for three minutes, and then a *down* position for five minutes, in a group of other dogs while you are out of view.

Utility Exercises (three passes earn the Utility Dog (UD) title)
- Heeling, coming, standing, sitting, downing, and staying in response to hand signals.
- Allowing the judge to touch him while the handler is 10 feet (3 m) away.
- Retrieving a leather, and then a metal, article scented by the handler from a group of similar unscented articles.
- Retrieving one of three gloves designated by the handler.
- Trotting away from the handler until told to stop and turn around 40 feet (12 m) away, and then jumping the designated jump and returning to the handler. This is then repeated, jumping the opposite jump.

    Novice. The Novice Standard class uses 12 to 13 obstacles, and the Novice JWW class uses 13 to 15 obstacles. The obstacles are set up in a fairly straightforward course. Dogs that qualify three times earn the Novice Agility (NA) or Novice Agility Jumpers (NAJ) titles, respectively.
    Open. The Open Standard class uses 15 to 17 obstacles, and the Open JWW class uses 16 to 18 obstacles, set up in a trickier pattern than in Novice. Dogs that qualify three times earn the Open Agility (OA) or Open Agility Jumpers (OAJ) titles, respectively.

Excellent. Both Excellent classes use 18 to 20 obstacles, set up in a very challenging pattern. Dogs that qualify three times earn the Agility Excellent (AX) or Agility Excellent Jumpers (AXJ) titles. Dogs that continue to compete in Excellent, and earn 10 additional qualifying scores by finishing the course in a slightly shorter time than required for the AX and AXJ titles, earn the Master Agility (MA) and Master Agility Jumpers (MAJ) titles.

Master Agility Champion (MACH). The MACH title is earned by qualifying at 20 trials in both standard and Jumpers Excellent classes, and earning 750 points. One point is earned for each second by which the dog beats the allotted course time.

Conformation

If your Yorkie is more the beauty pageant type, you may wish to try conformation dog showing. Pedigree is important here; unless your Yorkie comes from a family of show dogs, with Champions (designated by a "Ch" in front of their names) within the first few generations, chances are that he may not have the breeding required to meet the exacting points of the Yorkshire Terrier standard (page 169). If your breeder doesn't compete in dog shows, she probably did not choose your dog's parents with an eye toward producing a show dog. If, however, the breeder does compete in shows, ask her if she thinks your dog is competitive.

Fun Facts

Smartest in the Land

Six Yorkies have earned the OTCH title. The first was a dog named Thomas.

CHECKLIST

The AKC Agility Obstacles

✔ The A-frame is made of two 8- or 9-foot-long (2.4 or 2.7 m) boards, each 3 to 4 feet (about 1 m) wide, leaned against each other so they form an A-frame with the peak 5 to 5½ feet (1.5 to 1.7 m) off the ground. The dog runs up one side and down the other.

✔ The Dog Walk is either an 8- or 12-foot-long (2.4 or 3.6 m) and 1-foot-wide (30 cm) board that is either 3 or 4 feet high, suspended between two like boards that lead up to it on one side and down from it on the other. The dog runs up one plank, over the horizontal plank, and down the other plank.

✔ The Teeter is a seesaw with a 12-foot (3.6 m) plank. The dog runs up one side until his weight causes the teeter to shift so the dog can walk down the other side.

✔ The Pause Table is about 3 feet (about 1 m) square. The dog has to jump up on it, then either sit or lie down as commanded for 5 seconds.

✔ The Open Tunnel is a flexible tube, from 10 to 20 feet (3 to 6 m) in length and about 2 feet (61 cm) in diameter. It is often bent into an S or C shape for the dog to run through.

✔ The Chute is a rigid barrel with a light-weight fabric chute about 12 to 15 feet (3.6 to 4.6 m) long attached to one end. The dog runs into the open end of the barrel and continues blindly through the collapsed chute until he comes out the other end.

✔ The Weave Poles are a series of from 6 to 12 vertical poles spaced 20 to 24 inches (51 to 61 cm) apart. The dog takes a serpentine route weaving from one side of the poles to the other.

✔ The Jumps consist of single bar, panel, double bar, and triple bar jumps. The double and triples are both wide and tall, but all jumps are appropriately sized according to the dog's height. The bars are easily displaced, making it safe when a dog fails to clear them. The dog must jump without knocking any bars down.

✔ The Tire Jump is about 2 feet (61 cm) in diameter, with the bottom of the opening at the same height as the other jumps. The dog must jump through the opening.

✔ The Broad Jump is a spaced series of four to five slightly raised boards.

If your Yorkie is neutered or spayed, or has an AKC limited registration, he cannot be shown at AKC conformation shows. The breeder is the only person who can change the limited registration to regular registration, so her opinion is once again the first one you should seek.

Coat care is essential for a show Yorkie, so be prepared for a commitment to keeping the coat long and healthy (see Chapter Eight). You will also need to learn to present your Yorkie in the ring. Often a local kennel club, which you can locate through the AKC, will sponsor conformation handling classes

where you can practice posing and gaiting your dog. Your Yorkie will pose in the ring both on a table and on the ground. To pose your dog in a show pose, place his front legs roughly parallel to each other and perpendicular to the ground, and his rear legs also parallel to one another with the hocks (the area from the rear ankle to the foot) perpendicular to the ground. It takes a lot of practice and a lot of treats to get him to keep his feet where you put them. First try requiring him to stay still for only a second or so before rewarding him, gradually requiring him to stay longer before he gets the treat. He'll also need to trot next to you in a straight line. More important than getting everything perfect is doing it all with a happy attitude; you can help him keep this merry outlook through liberal handouts of treats.

Fun Facts

Jumping Yorkie!
The highest-titled agility Yorkie in history is MACH7 Desmond Aloysius Shelby, CD. The MACH7 indicates that he repeated the requirements for a MACH title seven times!

At a show, a judge will evaluate your Yorkie with regard to type—that is, how well he exemplifies the areas of the standard (see page 169) that define a Yorkshire Terrier as a Yorkshire Terrier, areas such as head shape, coat, and overall proportions. He will also be evaluated on soundness, his ability to

125

FYI: Tracking Title Requirements

A Champion Tracker (CT) title is given to a dog who has earned the TD, TDX, and VST titles. For more information, visit *www.akc.org/events/tracking*.

Title	Track length	Turns	Track age	Surface
Tracking Dog (TD)	440–500 yards	3–5	0.5–2 hours	natural
Tracking Dog Excellent (TDX)	800–1000 yards	5–7	3–5 hours	varied natural
Variable Surface (VST)	600–800 yards	4–8	3–5 hours	varied natural and manmade

walk or trot in as efficient a manner as possible. Finally, he'll be evaluated on temperament, checking that he is neither shy, aggressive, nor sulking.

If he ranks high in comparison to his competition, he may win from 1 to 5 points (of the 15 required) toward his championship, depending on how many dogs he's defeated.

Even if you leave the show ribbonless, you'll have lots of company; just don't let your Yorkie know and make sure you enjoy the day for what it should be: a fun outing with your dog where you can meet other Yorkie lovers. You may not always have the best dog in the judge's opinion, but you have the best one in your opinion, and the one you most want to take home.

Tracking

Although a Yorkie isn't what comes to mind when thinking of a search dog or even a drug detection dog, your Yorkie has an acute sense of smell capable of doing either task. If your Yorkie turns out to have a knack for following a track, he can earn various tracking titles offered by the AKC. Yorkies do have it rough compared to other breeds, as they must sometimes plow their way through comparatively high grass, but on the other hand, they are right next to the scent!

Fun Facts

Earthdog!

Yorkies were bred to hunt vermin, but few Yorkies have that sort of chance these days. With Earthdog events, the American Working Terrier Association gives them that opportunity in a safe environment where no animals are hurt. The dog is released near a manmade tunnel entrance and expected to enter the tunnel, follow it to the rat, and then mark the find by scratching, barking, or otherwise letting you know. The first Yorkie to earn that association's Certificate of Gameness was a dog by the name of Mr. Cinnamon T. Bun, AX MXJ NAC OAJ NAW TBAD CG CGC. The AKC also conducts Earthdog trials, but as of yet, does not allow Yorkies to compete in them.

ACTIVITIES Tracking Games

You can see for yourself how good your Yorkie's sense of smell is by trying a few scent games at home. Rub your scent on a ball and throw it into a pile of other balls. At first let your dog see it land, and then have him search for it without seeing exactly where it went. Either way, he should be able to bring you the same ball you tossed.

Another game you can play inside is to hide dog treats around the room. At first let him watch you hide them, and don't hide them too well. Then make him wait in the next room as you hide them, and hide them under furniture or in remote areas. This is a fun way for a Yorkie to work for his supper, which is especially good for dogs that eat too fast or too much. Just hide kibble instead of treats.

You can teach him to track with just a little more work. One way is to find an area you haven't walked over recently, and without your dog, walk a short distance, dropping treats along the trail. Then go get him and let him follow from treat to treat. Then repeat it in another fresh area, dropping the treats slightly farther apart. Eventually he'll figure out he can find the treats by following your scent trails, and you can leave a cache of treat treasure at the end of the trail.

You can also simply hide from him, assuming he wants to find you! This works best if you have a helper hold him while you go hide, walking over fresh ground and hiding in a bush or other covered area. Greet him with lots of praise and a few treats!

Travel Tips

Whether you have a competition to go to or just enjoy traveling for the sake of it, travel with your Yorkie can be fun as long as you make the proper preparations. Yorkies are great copilots, calm enough to travel quietly, active enough to enjoy excursions to see the sights, and small enough that you don't have to plan your next car purchase around them. But taking any dog on a car trip requires some planning. You'll need to find motels that allow dogs, and you'll need to make plans for keeping him safe and comfortable when you stop to eat, shop, or sightsee.

Car Travel

Just as you wear a seatbelt in the car, your Yorkie needs to be secured in case of an accident. Otherwise he can strike the dashboard, or you, or be ejected from the car. Even in minor accidents, a car door can pop open and the dog can panic and run away, never to be found. The best place for your Yorkie to ride is in a crate that is securely fastened to the inside of your car. Car seats for dogs, with harnesses to hold them in place, are also an option. Although not as safe as a crate, they are safer than letting the dog ride loose. As an extra safety measure, place emergency information on the side of the crate that says something like, "In case of emergency, take this dog to a veterinarian, then contact the following persons. Payment of all expenses incurred is guaranteed." Include any medications or health problems your dog may have. You may not always be able to speak for your dog after an accident.

Of course, your dog should be wearing identification as well, and not just your home phone number. If you're on vacation, add a contact number of somebody back home or where you can be reached.

Cooling an Overheated Dog. Don't plunge an overheated dog into ice water. This causes the peripheral blood vessels to contract, actually trapping the overheated blood at the body's core—just where it does most harm. Instead,

CAUTION

Killer Cars

Never leave your Yorkie inside a parked car in warm weather. Studies show that the temperature inside cars can reach lethal heights within 30 minutes, even if the weather outside is relatively cool. Regardless of outside air temperature, cars heat up at a fairly constant rate—gaining 80 percent of their final temperature within 30 minutes. Cars that start at a comfortable 72°F (22°C), for example, soar to a deadly 117°F (47°C) after 60 minutes in the sun. Cracking the windows scarcely affects the temperature inside. By padlocking your dog in a crate, and padlocking the crate to your car, you can buy a few minutes to run inside a rest stop on a hot day. You can use battery-operated fans aimed within the crate to help keep him cool. Ice packs—or, better, one of the cooling pads made for dogs using water-retaining gel pellets—can also help keep things cool. But don't rely on any such measures on a hot day. Of course, the best plan is to travel with another person and take turns staying with your dog. When possible, bring him along with you inside his carrier.

cool the dog slowly by placing him in cool water, or by draping him with wet towels and aiming a fan at him. Offer him plenty of cool water. If you have a thermometer, cool him until his temperature reaches 103° F (39° C), then stop, as it will continue to decline. As soon as you have him cooling, race him to the veterinarian. Even if he appears to have recovered, he needs to go to the veterinarian because some delayed but deadly effects can still occur even days later.

Air Travel

Because of his small size, your Yorkie can probably ride with you in the passenger section instead of the baggage compartment when flying. He must ride in a crate that can fit under the seat in front of you, and you must make reservations well in advance. He must stay in the crate throughout the flight.

CHECKLIST

Things to Pack

✔ Food and water bowls

✔ Food. If you use cans, get ones with pop tops or bring a can opener.

✔ Corn syrup (for dogs susceptible to hypoglycemia).

✔ Chewies and interactive toys to pass the time

✔ Bottled water or water from home. Strange water can sometimes cause diarrhea.

✔ Travel crate with bed

✔ Towels, including one to place over his bedding in the crate in case he gets carsick

✔ Paper towels, moist towelettes, rinse-free shampoo—that carsick thing again

✔ Medications, including anti-diarrhea and possibly his monthly heartworm preventive

✔ Bug spray or flea spray, possibly a flea comb

✔ Safe collar or harness with identification

✔ Short and long leashes

✔ Flashlight for late-night walks, or puppy pee-pee pads

✔ Plastic baggies or other poop disposal means

✔ Rabies certificate (some places require them)

✔ Recent color photo in case he gets lost

This is one time you may want to go easy on the food and water before you leave. Bring an absorbent puppy housetraining pad with you. If the situation becomes desperate, you can take the dog and the pad to the rest-room, disposing of the pad as you would a baby's diaper. Although you don't want to give too much food and water, some ice cubes and a few treats or a chewy can help the time pass more comfortably for him.

Motel Manners

Finding a motel that accepts pets is your first challenge. It's always a good idea to call ahead to make sure, and be prepared to pay a pet fee. To keep pets welcome at motels in the future, be sure you follow these rules:

- Bring his crate, or at least his own dog bed, in the room with you. If he gets on the bed, bring a sheet or roll down the bedspread so he doesn't get hair on it.
- Never leave your dog unattended in the room. He could feel deserted and try to dig his way out the door, or simply bark the whole time. Worse, somebody could let him out.
- If he has an accident on the carpet, don't try to hide it. Clean what you can and tell the management. Leave a big tip for housecleaning.
- Don't wash food bowls in the sink. The food clogs the drain.
- Don't wash your dog in the sink. The hair clogs the drain.
- Clean up any dog poop your dog deposits on the grounds.
- Be considerate of others. Don't let your dog bark!

Staying at Home

Sometimes leaving your Yorkie behind when you go out of town is the smartest choice you can make. If your dog has no issues being away from home, a boarding kennel is usually a good choice. The ideal kennel is approved by the American Boarding Kennel Association, and has climate-controlled accommodations and private runs for each dog that do not allow them to poke parts of themselves into adjacent runs. A caretaker should be on the grounds 24 hours a day. Ask to see the facilities. Most runs should be clean. It won't smell like apple pie, but it shouldn't make you lose your lunch. Good kennels require proof of current immunizations and an incoming check for fleas. They allow you to bring your dog's toys and bedding, and provide a raised area so that dogs don't have to sleep on the floor.

Helpful Hints

Online Travel Resources

www.1clickpethotels.com

www.aaa.com

www.canineauto.com

www.dogfriendly.com

www.doggonefun.com

www.fidofriendly.com

www.petsonthego.com

www.takeyourpet.com

www.travelpet.com

www.travelpets.com

Your veterinary office may also provide boarding facilities. They are often not as spacious as regular boarding kennels, but that's not necessarily a big deal for a Yorkie. This is your best choice for a dog who has ongoing health problems.

Pet sitters offer yet another choice. Bonded, experienced pet sitters are a better choice than the kid next door because they're responsible and are usually trained to spot signs of trouble. The main drawback is that they can usually only visit a couple of times a day, a potential problem for a dog susceptible to hypoglycemia, and also a problem unless your dog is paper- or litter box-trained.

Finally, some individuals offer in-home boarding for a limited number of dogs. The dogs essentially live as the host's dog for the time they are visiting. This provides a comfortable environment for your dog, but make sure the home is safe for your little dog first, and that large dogs won't also be boarded and loose at the same time.

Finding a Lost Dog

If your Yorkie is missing, don't wait to see if he'll come back. The sooner you organize your search, the better your chances of recovering him. If your dog has just disappeared, begin your search by going first to the place your dog would most likely go, which is usually a place he has been to before, and to the most dangerous place your dog could go, which is usually a roadway. Be careful that your calling doesn't lure your dog across a road.

If you are not able to find your dog quickly, your time is best spent getting the word out and convincing others to help you search. Call friends and neighbors to help. Many jobs need to be performed.

- Continue the foot search; call on friends, or consider hiring helpers from scout troops or local college or high school job boards. Also contact local kennel clubs and training classes for helpers. Be careful, though. Too many searchers may actually scare timid dogs. Strange people calling him or, worse, trying to catch him, can send even a confident dog into a panic to the point that he won't even come to you. If the dog is in a safe area, searchers should keep an eye on him from a distance and wait for you to arrive. Remember, also, that a dog who is caught in something may bark or whine but will usually become quiet when he hears voices calling. Searchers should be sure to be quiet for long periods.
- Ask area delivery people, children, and neighbors if they have seen a dog matching yours.
- Call area veterinarians to see if an injured Yorkie has been brought in.
- Call area shelters. Even if they say no such dog has been brought in, visit them by the following day. Keep checking.
- Make large posters to saturate the area. The poster should state in large red letters "REWARD." Include the amount of the reward you plan to offer if $100 or more, and specify "for information leading to the return of this lost dog." The larger the reward, the more interest it will attract. Include a photo of the dog and a large phone number. Place the posters at every intersection so people in stopped cars can read them. At traffic lights, place several along the line where cars will be stopped. Also place posters at eye level along sidewalks and anyplace people pass by at a slow pace. Some large pet supply stores sell rolls of plastic "fill in the blank" Lost Dog posters.
- Ask to place posters or fliers in all area grooming shops, pet supply stores, veterinary clinics, animal shelters, convenience stores, Laundromats, grocery stores, and other high-traffic places. Also ask to post them in local schools.
- Hand out fliers to neighbors. Make mailer postcards for delivery in a larger target area (2- to 5-mile radius from the place your dog was lost) and to veterinary clinics and animal shelters. Note that some national organizations, such as www.sherlockbones.com (1-800-942-6637), can help you prepare posters and pre-addressed mailers (depending on your location) and deliver them to you by overnight mail for a fee.
- Take out a classified ad in the newspaper. Choose the paper with the largest circulation. Don't be too specific about the area in which your dog was lost because if he's spotted elsewhere people may assume it's not him. Don't mention the dog is valuable or a beloved family pet. Some cruel people use such ads as ways to upset you by calling and saying terrible things just to hear your reaction. Don't give the dog's

name. Do say the dog needs medication. Check the ad for accuracy. Check the found ads in all regional papers.

- Call the non-emergency number for the local police agencies and ask that patrolling officers be on the lookout for the dog.
- If your dog was lost while away from home, you need to provide him with something familiar where he last saw you. Many dogs will return to the place they were last with their owner. If possible, keep your car parked there with a door open. If your dog sleeps in a crate, leave it where he was last seen. Always leave articles with your fresh scent on them in the area. Make sure that, if your dog returns, he doesn't feel like you've left him.
- If your dog was lost near an interstate, find somebody with a CB radio and ask him or her to get the word out to truck drivers.
- Call local radio stations and try to have them announce the lost dog.
- Contact area school bus drivers.
- Get the word out on Internet groups.
- Contact the city or county road cleanup crews to find if they have removed any dogs hit by cars. As sad as that ending is, it's better than never knowing if your dog is still lost.

Don't give up hope. Many dogs have been found days, weeks, and sometimes even months after they've been lost. But the less time that elapses before you mobilize your search, the greater your chances are of recovery. This is one time it pays to be an alarmist, and one of many times it pays to be prepared. And remember, it always pays to have an identification microchip in your dog!

CAUTION

Cold Weather Warning

Yorkies are also susceptible to hypothermia and frostbite in cold weather. Several factors affect how well a dog can deal with cold temperatures.

- **Hair:** The Yorkie's hair, though long, is actually thin compared to other breeds, with fewer hair follicles and very little undercoat. As a result, it doesn't keep them very warm. Your Yorkie will appreciate a store-bought coat in cold weather.
- **Size:** Dogs amass body heat according to volume, and lose it according to surface area. The Yorkie's small body loses more body heat than a big dog, comparatively.
- **Health:** Dogs with poor health or nutrition lack the resistance that healthy dogs have. They may also lack body fat, which is a valuable source of insulation.
- **Age:** Very young or very old dogs are very likely to lack appropriate fat for insulation, and tend to be more prone to hypothermia.

Snow and ice can form into little balls inside a dog's paws, so you need to check them regularly. Salt and de-icing chemicals can irritate paws, and can even be toxic if your dog licks them off his paws. You can prevent these problems by having him wear booties.

Leash Training

1 Place a leash on the puppy, and without pulling on it, lure him forward a step or two with a treat. Give him the treat. Keep luring him forward a little more and more as you walk slowly along with him at your side, giving him the treat every few steps.

2 If he wants to go in a different direction, let him lead for a few steps before trying to lure him along again.

3 If he refuses to move, pick him up and carry him away a few steps, then put him down and start over. Just don't let him dupe you into carrying him everywhere!

4 If he pulls ahead on the leash, pulling you, just stop. Only when he lets the leash go slack do you say "Good!" and reward or move forward.

The *Sit* Command

1 With him sitting with his back to a corner, hold a treat just above and behind the level of his eyes. If he bends his knees and points his nose up, say "Good!" and give him the treat.

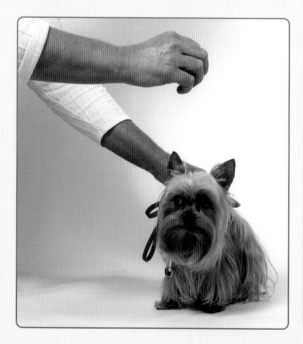

2 The next time, move the treat farther back so he has to bend his legs more to get it. Keep repeating and moving it back until he's sitting. Be sure to tell him he's good right away and give him the treat each time.

3 Now guide him using just your hand with no treat. When he sits, give him a treat from your other hand.

4 Gradually abbreviate your hand movements until you are only using a small hand signal. Then add the verbal signal "Sit!" right before the hand signal. Keep practicing and rewarding him.

The *Stay* Command

1 Have him sit beside you, then say "Stay" while holding your palm in a "stop" signal in front of his face. If he gets up, simply put him back in position and start over, decreasing the duration you expect of him. Wait for a few seconds, then reward him and say "OK!"

2 After he's doing this reliably, do it again except, this time, pivot so you're standing facing him. Wait for a few seconds, then reward him and say "OK!"

3 Next, work on moving around so you are on either side of and even behind your dog, and then gradually increase the distance, then time.

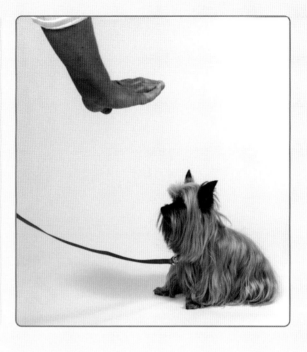

4 Introduce mild distractions, then practice in other locations. Keep him on a long line if you're anywhere he could get loose.

Chapter Eight

Grooming

The Yorkshire Terrier that moves across the show ring glides like a parade float, his legs hidden by a mantle of flowing tresses of gunmetal steel and liquid gold. That coat doesn't come easy, but with good care your Yorkie can look like that, or close to it. Of course, you're going to need a little guidance and a lot of dedication.

You won't need nearly as much of either if you decide that a cute short clip is more to your liking. After all, that's what most show dogs get after they retire from the ring. The short coat still takes some work, but it's fairly easy to put the hard part of the job into a groomer's hands.

The long and the short of it, though, is that one of the best parts of the Yorkie's coat is how it feels. When well groomed, it's satiny and cool to the touch, a joy to caress as your dog sits on your lap. That, too, requires some diligence, because no matter the length, a Yorkie's coat must first of all be clean and healthy.

This chapter will tell you how to keep any length coat clean, tangle-free, and healthy. It will also give you tips on growing a long coat and choices if you've decided a short coat is for you. While professional groomers may play a large role in your dog's grooming, everyday grooming is just as important. If you get started right, both you and your Yorkie will come to look forward to your grooming sessions as a special relaxing time together.

Breed Truths

Coat Texture and Length

Some Yorkie coats grow longer and shine more than others. Show breeders strive for such satiny coats, but not all Yorkies have them. Some have a more cottony texture, which looks fuller and tends to tangle and break more easily. Although the cottony type is harder to grow to great lengths, with good care you can help any coat be all that it can be.

Ten Steps to Growing a Long Coat

1. **Maintain good health.** Systemic health problems can adversely affect your dog's skin, which is his largest organ, and, in turn, his coat. In some cases of generalized illness, hair growth is slowed or stopped as the body's resources are focused elsewhere. The hair enters a dormant phase in which it is more easily shed, which is one reason sick dogs tend to shed more. New hair may be slow to come, and when it does, the hair cuticle may be abnormal, resulting in a dull, dry coat. If your dog's coat suddenly becomes sparse or brittle, it may be a sign that a checkup is needed.

2. **Provide good nutrition.** Hair is made up of about 95 percent protein. All told, if you added up how much hair grows from an average dog's follicles, it would amount to about 100 feet of hair a day! That hair, plus the constant replacement of skin cells, uses about 25 to 30 percent of a dog's daily protein requirement. If your dog's diet lacks protein, it's going to show up in poor hair growth and poor-quality hair that is rough, brittle, and easily broken. Hair also requires essential fatty acids, vitamin B complex, vitamin C, vitamin E, and minerals such as zinc, among others. You can buy several supplements specially formulated to include nutrients helpful to coat growth. To find examples, search the Internet for "hair on a doorknob." Overall, your best bet is to feed a well-balanced diet with fairly high protein that includes omega fatty acids (especially omega-3, which has the additional benefit of slightly reducing inflammatory skin responses to allergens) and vitamins B, C, E, A, and K. If you change foods, keep an eye on your dog's coat and if it starts to look poor, find another food, or see your veterinarian.

3. **Eradicate parasites.** Internal parasites can destroy all your efforts at good nutrition. External parasites can cause hair loss through itching that leads to scratching and chewing. Fleas can also cause fleabite dermatitis, in which the flea's saliva creates a widespread allergic reaction and itching. Mites can invade hair follicles and cause the hairs to fall out.

4. **Comb daily.** Little snarls become big tangles, which become solid mats. It's almost impossible to remove mats without losing hair. It's especially important to comb after nature walks, or if your Yorkie has a yard with lots of greenery, because small twigs and burrs tend to get hair wrapped around them, causing instant tangles. Use a pin brush or a wide-toothed comb. If you use a pin brush, don't use the type with little balls at the end of each pin, as these can pull the coat. Do not use a nylon, natural-bristle, or slicker brush. Mist the coat with coat conditioner before combing, and use a steel comb to gently work through the hair.

5. **Bathe often.** As oil accumulates down the hair shaft, it attracts dirt, and the combination changes the hair texture so that it tends to

cling, tangle, and mat. If you really want a show-dog coat, plan to bathe your dog at least once a week.

6. **Spot-bathe problem areas.** Organic materials such as food, blood, and feces will rot, and if these materials are clinging to your dog's hair, they will rot the hair along with them. Other body products, such as saliva, urine, and eye discharge, may be acidic or contain enzymes that break down hair. Rather than bathe the entire dog, use a rinse-free shampoo to keep these areas clean, or do a quick spot-bath.

7. **Avoid excessive heat.** If you're blow-drying, use the lowest heat setting possible. Better yet, invest in a forced-air dryer, which uses cool air blown at high speed to dry.

8. **Avoid abrasive surfaces.** It makes sense that letting your Yorkie run through thickets and thorns is a surefire way to destroy his coat, but you may not think about things inside your house. You really do have an excuse to use satin sheets; slick surfaces are the least harmful for long, delicate hair. Even carpeting can be damaging to Yorkie coats.

9. **Use protective wraps.** Wrap small sections of coat in wax or rice paper, fold it up, and band it. Wrapping keeps the coat from dragging on the ground or getting tangled.

10. **Don't leave clothes on.** Don't leave collars, harnesses, or cute outfits on your dog more than necessary. They can rub against the hair and break it.

HOME BASICS
Wrap It Up!

Show Yorkies don't always run around with their long tresses flowing behind them. Instead, their hair is wrapped up so it doesn't get dirty, tangled, or broken. It's a peculiar look, and more work than you'll want to go through unless you want a show coat, but here's how you do it.

You'll need a box of either doughnut paper, wax paper, or rice paper, and a package of tiny latex bands. The doughnut paper is easiest to use, and you can get it at bulk-buy stores. It's not as long as rice paper, which is needed for drag-on-the-floor-length coats.

1. Divide the coat into small sections, each about an inch or so. Place a latex band in each section about an inch from the skin. Make sure your dog can move without the banded hair pulling on the skin.
2. Fold your papers into thirds lengthwise, with the waxed part on the outside, facing away from the coat. You may wish to cut off or fold under any serrated edges first, as these can cut the coat.
3. Place one coat section in the middle third section of one paper.
4. Fold each side of the paper over the coat section.
5. Fold the paper with hair inside upon itself two to three times, so it's close to the body.
6. Place a latex band around the middle of the paper to secure it, making sure the band isn't on the hair.
7. Using scissors, carefully snip out the first latex band you put in.
8. Move on to the next section.
9. Check every day to make sure the wraps aren't pulling, or that mats aren't forming beneath them.
10. Remove and repeat the process every few days, or immediately if the hair and wraps get wet.

Skin Care

You can't expect your Yorkie to have long, shiny hair if the hair is growing out of itchy, inflamed skin. More important, your Yorkie is going to be uncomfortable. As your dog's largest organ, and most visible one, skin, and its problems, are nothing to dismiss.

If your Yorkie is scratching, chewing, rubbing, and licking, he may have allergies, perhaps to inhaled allergens, or things he comes in contact with, like foods or fleas. Unlike humans, where hay fever and other inhaled allergens typically cause sneezing, in dogs they more often cause itching. Food, too, can cause allergies. Signs of allergies are typically reddened itchy skin, particularly around the ears, eyes, feet, forelegs, armpits, and abdomen. The dog may scratch and lick, and rub his torso or rump on furniture or rugs.

Allergens can be isolated with a skin test, in which small amounts of allergen extracts are injected under the skin, which is then monitored for reactions. Besides simply avoiding allergens, some treatments are available.

The most common inhaled allergens are dander, pollen, dust, and mold. They are often seasonal. Signs most commonly appear between 1 and 3 years of age. Treatment includes antihistamines, glucocorticoids, and hyposensitization.

The most common allergy among all dogs is flea allergy dermatitis (FAD), which is an allergic reaction to the saliva that a flea injects under the skin whenever it feeds. Not only does it cause intense itching in that area but all over the dog, especially around the rump, legs, and paws. Even a single fleabite can cause severe reactions in allergic dogs. The cure? Get rid of fleas.

Stop the Itch!

Everybody has an occasional itch. But persistent itching, or itching accompanied by vigorous chewing or rubbing, or by inflamed or broken skin, is more than a casual itch. It's a sign of a skin problem, one that will only get worse. That's because itching and chewing further damage the skin, creating a swampy welcome center for bacteria to compound the initial problem.

Yorkies can itch for many reasons, so your best bet is to get your veterinarian's opinion. Meanwhile, you can try some home treatments.

Start simple. Apply an ice pack to the affected area. Or for a larger area, try a cool-water dip, immersing the dog in water for ten minutes. Pat dry, avoiding blow-drying or vigorous rubbing.

Bathing may give better results. But remember, any medicated shampoo must be in contact with the skin for at least ten minutes in order to be effective. And use cool water! Consider these products:

- Colloidal oatmeal products draw inflammatory toxins from the skin, reducing itchiness for up to three days. They come in soaks, shampoos, and crème rinses, with the latter having the longest-lasting effects. Some colloidal oatmeal products are combined with local anesthetics to further sooth the skin.
- Bath oils added to the water may help moisturize overly dry skin.
- Flea shampoos can kill fleas, but if you don't have a flea shampoo, almost any shampoo will kill them. Just leave it on a little longer.
- Lime-sulfur shampoos are good for drying weeping skin lesions and alleviating itchiness. They also kill some parasites and bacteria. Warning: They smell horrible and can stain fur and clothing!
- Antiseptic soaps and shampoos are effective on broken skin, especially hot spots and puppy impetigo. Even antiseptic mouthwash will help.

After bathing, you may wish to apply one of the following topical sprays or ointments.

- Witch hazel spray or lotion has a cooling effect that may be soothing in some cases.
- Moisturizer sprays or dips can help alleviate the itchiness of overly dry skin.

- Aloe vera contains enzymes that break down inflammatory proteins. Most aloe vera products are mixed with other ingredients that render them less effective and possibly harmful to dogs that lick them off. Pure aloe vera is available from most health food stores.
- Anti-itch sprays and creams for humans can be soothing to dogs. Avoid calamine lotion, though. It can make dogs sick if they lick it off. Always read the labels of any products made for humans because they are not designed for use on an animal that might ingest them. If it says it is poisonous, do not use it unless you can prevent your Yorkie from licking it.
- Topical steroid sprays and creams can provide fast relief from itching without the untoward side effects of oral steroids.

In severe cases, bathing and topical applications may not be enough to give your puppy relief. Oral drugs and supplements may be helpful.

- Oral antihistamines are commonly prescribed by veterinarians to quell itching. Histamines can cause inflammation in dogs, but not to the extent they do in humans. Thus, antihistamines may not be as effective in dogs. Some may be more effective than others, but finding the correct one usually takes a couple of weeks of trials for each antihistamine. They are likely to cause drowsiness, which may be a desirable side effect in cases of intense itching, but not for long-term use. Commonly used antihistamines are clemastine fumarate, diphenhydramine, chlorphenamine, and hydroxyzine. It is extremely important that any over-the-counter antihistamines given to a dog not contain other medications, such as those found in sinus or cold relief medications. Talk to your veterinarian ahead of time to find out the correct dosage for your puppy or adult dog, and keep some in the medicine chest.
- Fatty acid supplementation isn't a quick solution, but it can provide improvement over the long term. It's effective in up to one quarter of cases of itchy skin, especially when used in conjunction with antihistamines. Do not confuse these supplements with those sold as food supplements to improve coat quality. Fish oil is one good source of fatty acids.

Finally, try to get your Yorkie's mind off the itch. Play some games, go for a walk, or give a treat that requires extensive chewing or working. If the scratching and biting continue, try covering his trunk with a little doggy T-shirt or his feet with doggie booties. An Elizabethan collar, available from your veterinarian and some pet supply stores, can prevent the pup from scratching his face and chewing parts of his body—but he'll despise wearing it!

If itching continues, take your Yorkie to the veterinarian for diagnosis and treatment. Severe itching may call for oral cortisone medication. This provides the most immediate and effective relief, and may be necessary in order to start treating the condition. If your Yorkie still has skin problems, consider consulting a veterinary dermatologist, which you can locate through the American College of Veterinary Dermatology at *www.acvd.org/public/findaderm*.

Parasite Control

The fastest way to ruin a nice coat, besides cutting it off, is to let your Yorkie get parasites so he can scratch and chew it off. A parasite-free dog is more comfortable, and certainly more pleasant to hold and pet. Controlling fleas and ticks and mites used to be a non-stop job, but newer products now make it comparatively easy.

Fleas. Fighting fleas used to mean treating your dog, his bedding, your house, and your yard, along with daily vacuuming and flea combing. No wonder the fleas won. Now dog owners have options that are easy and effective.

The best course of action is to vary the type of flea product you use, so that fleas have less chance of becoming resistant. For example, use imidacloprid one month, fipronil another, and metaflumizone another. You can also use them in conjunction with lufenuron to prevent fleas from reproducing. Most of these products are available only from your veterinarian, and although they cost more than the traditional flea sprays you can buy in the grocery story, they're

CAUTION

Beyond the Bite

Fleas and ticks not only cause intense itching and scratching, but fleas can cause flea allergy dermatitis and tapeworms, and ticks can cause ehrlichiosis, babesia, and Lyme disease, among others. Your veterinarian can order blood tests if these conditions are suspected. And be careful yourself; you can catch some of the same diseases from exposure to these parasites.

FYI: Flea Treatments

Ingredient	Application	Action
Imidacloprid	spot-on, 1–3 months	kills 98% of fleas in 1 hour; continues for 1 month
Fipronil	spray, spot-on, 1–3 months	kills fleas, and to a lesser extent, ticks for 1–3 months
Lufenuron	pill, monthly	renders fleas that bite the dog sterile
Pyriproxifen	spray, every 3 months	renders fleas that bite the dog sterile
Selamectin	spot-on, monthly	kills and sterilizes fleas; prevents heartworms
Nitenpyram	pill, as needed	instantly kills fleas; no residual action
Metaflumizone	spot-on, monthly	kills fleas in 48 hours; continues for 1 month
Amitraz	spot-on, collar, monthly	kills ticks for up to 1 month
Permethrin	spray, spot-on, as needed	kills fleas, and to a lesser extent, ticks; no residual action

worth it. They're safer, more effective, and because they have residual action, you'll spend far less money in the long run.

Ticks. Ticks are persistent pests, but they, too, are gradually being beaten by newer products. Still, the old-fashioned way of dealing with ticks is worth knowing. If you're in tick territory, examine your dog in the tick-favored spots: on his ears, neck, withers, and between his toes. If you find one, use a tissue to grasp it as close to the skin as possible, and pull it straight out, without twisting or squeezing.

Mites. Mites can also cause problems. Sarcoptic mites cause sarcoptic mange, an intensely itchy disorder that you can catch (it's called scabies in people). It's often characterized by small bumps and crusts on the ear tips, abdomen, elbows, and hocks. The condition can be treated with repeated shampoos or with veterinary-prescribed drug treatment.

Demodex mites cause demodectic mange, a non-contagious but often difficult-to-treat condition. A couple of small patches in a puppy are commonplace and will usually go away on their own, but many such patches or a generalized condition must be treated with repeated dips or with drug therapy. Cases involving the feet can be especially difficult to cure.

Bathing Beauties

Your Yorkie will be a lot more pleasant to hold and pet if he's clean and fresh-smelling, and that means he needs regular baths, just as you do. For some reason, the myth got started years ago that bathing dogs too often is bad for their coats. Perhaps that's true if you use harsh shampoos, but keep in mind that show dogs are often bathed several times a week, and have gorgeous coats. In general, expect to wash your Yorkie every one to four weeks, depending on coat length and lifestyle.

CAUTION

Cage Drying

It's tempting to place your dog in a crate and aim a dryer at him. But it's also dangerous, especially in an enclosed crate. Many dogs have overheated like this when their owners forgot about them.

Although Yorkie hair feels much like human hair, Yorkie skin has a different pH (7.0 to 7.5) than human skin (5.5). Human shampoo will do an

HOME BASICS
How to Wash Your Yorkie

1. Remove all tangles and mats. Wet hair expands, which means any matted hair expands and gets matted even worse. And when it dries, it tends to shrink down into a more solid mat. Never bathe mats.

2. Check the ears and clean them if needed. Ear cleaner and debris tends to stick to the hair, so you'll want to wash it out.

3. Place your dog in the sink and wet him down, starting at his neck and working down and back. Lift the hair so it gets wet all the way to the skin. Wet his head last, using a sponge. Avoid getting water into his ears.

4. Put some shampoo in your palm and rub your hands together, then rub your hands all over the dog, repeating the process as needed when you need more shampoo. Use a tear-free shampoo around the face.

5. Gently massage to the skin, taking care not to twist, rub, or tangle the hair. You need not do any vigorous scrubbing or lathering, but you will get better results if you keep adding more water throughout the process. Thorough cleansing requires soap and water molecules to bind with one another, which can't happen if you don't have enough water in the mix.

6. Rinse the shampoo out entirely, starting at the head and working down and back. You can rinse the face with a sponge, which your Yorkie will prefer to being sprayed in the face.

7. Repeat the process using a coat conditioner instead of shampoo. Again, rinse thoroughly.

8. Gently squeeze the water from the coat, then cover your dog with a towel and place him somewhere to shake off what he can. Make sure he's in a place he can't slip down or run off, because dogs love to run amuck right after a bath. Then wrap him with an absorbent towel so it sucks up as much water as possible. You can also pat him dry, but don't rub, which will just tangle the hair.

9. Ideally, you should use a blow-dryer to finish drying him. It will give the hair a sleeker, flatter finish and will keep a wet dog from shivering on your furniture. You can use a human blow-dryer, but use one with the lowest heat setting possible. Get your Yorkie used to it gradually, first by blowing it near him, then so it just blows on him from a distance, and finally blowing parts of his coat dry a bit at a time. Most Yorkies grow to enjoy the process, although they may be skittish around the head. Never keep the air aimed at the same place long enough that it could burn the skin. Instead, work around the dog, saving the delicate areas, such as the face, ears, and under the tail, for last. You can use your fingers at first to separate the hair so it dries faster, and also monitor how hot the air is on his skin. When the hair changes from wet to damp, use a wide-tooth comb or a pin brush to gently brush the hair as you dry it.

10. Take a picture!

adequate job on most Yorkies, but if you really want to grow a long coat, or if your dog has any sort of skin problem, buy a high-quality dog shampoo.

The best place to wash your Yorkie is in a large sink with a hand sprayer. If you don't have a hand sprayer, use a cup to apply water rather than trying to hold your dog under the tap. Place a screen over the drain to catch any hair, and a non-slip mat or a towel at the bottom of the sink. Gather your supplies (shampoo, conditioner, sponge, towel) and adjust the water so it's lukewarm. Cold water doesn't allow the cuticle of the hair to open sufficiently for easy cleaning, and hot water can open it too much. More important, water that's too hot or cold is uncomfortable.

Brushing and Combing

Brushing your Yorkie will be easier if you keep on a schedule and follow a pattern—and if you get your equipment together before you get started. You'll need the following items

- Spritzer bottle with a mixture of ¼ coat conditioner and ¾ water
- Steel comb with wide and fine teeth
- Pin brush
- Detangling spray
- Towel

Once you've gathered your supplies, round up your dog, turn up the soothing music, and try to relax. Then follow these steps.

1. Place the dog on the towel and spritz the area you'll be working on until it's slightly damp. Never brush a dry coat, because it creates static electricity that causes tangles, and because a dry coat breaks more easily. Spritz down to the skin, lifting the coat in layers to reach it.
2. With the dog on his side, lift the coat up so you're looking at the hair that grows from the lower part of his body. Start brushing this lower coat first, beginning at the ends of the hair and working toward the skin. Use the pin brush first, then the wide-toothed comb, and finally the fine-toothed comb.
3. When the lower layer is tangle-free, brush the layer above it into place and repeat the process. Continue doing this, adding in additional top layers, until you reach the top of the dog.
4. Do the other side, or do the legs on the side you're on.
5. Do the head and tail.
6. You can vary the order, but just remember what you've done!

Mats. Oh what a tangled web we weave—when unbrushed the coat we do leave! It could be the start of a tragic epic, the tale of the unbrushed

Yorkie. That's because brushing is more than cosmetic. It's not uncommon for Yorkies to come into rescue or to groomers with coats so matted that they've caused health problems. One common problem occurs when the dog's rear end is never cleaned. Fecal matter gets caught in the coat and, the coat mats around it, until eventually the area is so matted that it entirely covers the anus, preventing proper defecation. Not only is this disgusting, but it can attract flies, which lay their eggs in the fecal matter that is now pressed into the skin, and maggots emerge and eat into the dog. If the mat is tight enough, it can cause impaction, preventing the dog from defecating because there's no place for the feces to go.

Mats on other parts of the body can cause other problems. Mats tend to grow and compress as they age, recruiting more hair from their margins and pulling it into an ever-tightening mass. As this happens, it also pulls the skin that the hair is attached to. At best, it causes the dog to be uncomfortable; at worst, it prevents the dog from even walking because its legs are matted into place. And again, the area below the mat holds moisture and bacteria, setting up a playground for infections that may only be visible once the mat is removed, but are certainly painful to the dog all along.

Make brushing a part of your daily routine, perhaps as you watch television at night. It's easiest if your Yorkie is trained to lie in your lap, on the sofa beside you, or on a table that's slightly higher than lap level. If you start early, your dog will look forward to these sessions and probably fall asleep during them. Start early with your puppy, using a soft brush and never pulling on tangles.

Breed Needs

Trimming the Anal Area

Some trimming is for looks, but trimming around the anal area is for cleanliness. If this is the only trimming you ever plan to do yourself, you can buy an inexpensive moustache trimmer and use it to clip the hair short in an area about a half inch or so around the anus. If you already have clippers, you can use a #10 blade for this. You can also use blunt-nosed scissors.

Coping with Tangles

Tangles and mats can appear anywhere, but happen most often in oily areas, such as behind the ears, or in friction areas, such as in the armpits. If it's a small knot, use your fingers to pull the hairs away. Spraying the tangle with a detangler can help. Next use the wide-toothed comb to try to comb hair out of the tangle or mat. Remember, comb the hair out of the mat, not the mat out of the hair. If the mat is large, you may need to split it lengthwise, pulling it apart with your fingers.

What about cutting the mat out? Sometimes that's the kindest solution, but you have to be extremely careful not to cut the skin. If you decide to use scissors to cut the mat lengthwise, or to simply cut it out, first wriggle a comb between the mat and the skin. When mats are tight, it's hard to tell where the mat ends and the skin begins, so the comb acts as a barrier. Of course, be sure to cut on the hair side, not the skin side, of the comb.

If the dog is extensively matted, you need an experienced professional groomer. Be forewarned that the skin beneath such matting is often already bruised, fragile, and unhealthy from the pulling and bacteria caused by the mats. But the dog will feel immensely better, and can then grow a new coat from scratch.

Some coats are more prone to tangling than others. The correct satiny coat is easier to maintain tangle-free than is the cottony coat some Yorkies have. If you feel like you're spending your entire life brushing and de-matting, try different conditioners and detanglers, and if that doesn't help, consider clipping the hair. It's no favor to either of you to maintain him in a coat that requires all that work. Besides, clips are cute!

How to Tie a Topknot

You'll need a comb, something to part the hair with such as a knitting needle or pencil, several small rubber bands, and a bow. It helps if your dog is taught to lie down with his chin resting on a small pillow while you work on him.

Here's how to make an everyday topknot:

1. Comb the hair on the head so it falls naturally.
2. Make a part from the outer corner of the eye to the inner corner of the ear on that side. Do the same on the other side.
3. Comb the hair upward and then backward between the ears.
4. Place a latex band near the base to hold it in place. You can add a bow or barrette to the latex band for looks.
5. Gently use the knitting needle to pull the hair in the area of the forehead forward so it's not pulled tight, but instead goes forward in a little pouf.
6. If your dog has long hair in his topknot, you can do this additional step, adding the bow afterward: Gather the long strand and fold it back on itself, placing another latex band over the same place as the first, this time with the additional piece tucked in. However, don't leave this in for long because the second latex band is more likely to break the coat.
7. Whenever you remove a latex band, cut it out, don't pull it out. Pulling it out almost always takes coat with it.

Cute Short Cuts

A Yorkshire Terrier with trailing tresses is one of the most eye-catching of dogs. It's also a lot of work. You may find that your schedule doesn't allow you to keep such a coat up properly, or that it's too restrictive for the activities you'd planned for your dog. Many people elect to keep their Yorkies trimmed to a more manageable length.

Pros:

- Clipped Yorkies are cute!
- Clipped Yorkies require less brushing, bathing, and drying time.
- Clipped Yorkies can go swimming and hiking.
- Clipped Yorkies are better able to compete in some sports such as agility.

Cons:

- Clipped Yorkies lack the traditional look of the breed.
- Clipped Yorkies can't compete in conformation dog shows.
- Clipped Yorkies require professional grooming, or practice on your part.
- Clipped Yorkies will require clipping every one to three months.

If you decide clipping is for you, you'll probably want to have a professional groomer do the job. This is a fairly common request, so most groomers will be able to give you a good idea of how your dog will look, and even some style options. One popular clip is basically a Schnauzer trim, in which the hair is left fairly long on the legs and face.

If you want to clip your dog yourself, it will take a few tries but eventually you'll get good at it. You may even want to pay a groomer or experienced breeder to give you some basic lessons.

You'll need the following equipment for a home clip job:

Clippers. Buy a good clipper. Cheap clippers don't cut well, and they can grab and pull the hair. Expect to pay over $100 for a decent clipper.

Snap-on blades. These snap on and off your clipper and enable it to trim to different lengths. Blades come labeled with different numbers; the higher the number, the closer the cut. Most clippers come with a #10 blade. You will also need either a #4, 5, 7, or 8½ blade, depending on how short you want the hair. The #4 will leave the hair about one or two inches long, whereas the #10 leaves it fairly close to the skin. Of course, the longer the hair, the sooner you have to clip it again. A #40 blade is optional; it's used to cut the hair on the tips of the ears, but you only need to do that if you want a show coat.

Snap-on combs. You can also buy comb attachments that fit over the blade and allow you to keep the hair slightly longer when you cut.

Blunt-nosed scissors.

Moustache trimmer. This is optional, but handy.

In general, if you cut in the direction of hair growth, you'll get a slightly longer cut that may sometimes leave lines in the hair. If you cut against the lay of the hair, you'll get a shorter, smoother cut, but you run a greater risk of making gouge marks. Don't worry; whatever you do can be fixed. The hair will always grow back! Of course, don't cut the dog's skin!

For all clips, start by using the #10 blade to clip the hair around the anus, between the thighs, around the genitals, and in the arm pits. You want the hair very short in these areas to prevent any fecal matter, urine, or dirt from getting in it, and to prevent matting in mat-prone areas.

Schnauzer Clip

1. Working from the top of the dog to the bottom and rear to the front, and going against the growth of the hair, use the #7 blade to clip all the blue hair away. Start at the base of the tail and the back of the legs, and work forward to the base of the skull and front of the chest. Clip the hair under the dog as well, including under the neck up to the head. This should leave the dog with short hair wherever his blue hair is, or with short hair on his body down to the level of his elbows and knees.
2. You may leave the hair long on the tail if you wish, or clip it as though it were part of the body.
3. Use scissors to trim around the foot pads and cut off any hair that drags on the floor.
4. Comb the hair around the face forward, and use scissors to cut the bangs just above the eyes. If you prefer, you can first form a topknot, and cut the rest of the hair around it, but leave the topknot intact.

5. Using your fingers to hold and measure the hair around the face, continue to comb it forward and cut it to the same length as the bangs, or a little longer, so that it frames the face in a circle, including the chin.
6. Angle back from the dog's nose at about a 45-degree angle, so the hair is shorter near the tip of the muzzle and gets gradually longer farther back, until it reaches the line between the head and neck on the sides.
7. Scissor the hair under the jaw so it gradually meets the short hair of the neck around the jaw line.

Puppy clip. Do exactly as you did for the Schnauzer clip, except use a #10 blade with a snap-on comb attachment. The body coat will be longer than with the Schnauzer clip.

How to Trim Yorkie Ears

It's important to keep the long hair on the upper part of your Yorkie's ears clipped short when he is a puppy. His ears are so thin that even that slight weight can tip them forward resulting in ears that never stand as an adult. On an adult, it's your choice whether you want them clipped, which is traditional, or whether you want to let them grow fluffy.

Experienced groomers use a #40 or #30 blade to get a nearly naked cut, but you're better off to start with a #15, which has less chance of nicking the fragile skin. Even better, just use a moustache trimmer. Always clip ears in the direction of hair growth—that is, from base toward tip, to avoid nicking. Place your finger on the opposite side of the ear to keep it steady as you clip.

1. Trim off the hair on the upper third of the ears, front and back.
2. On the rear side, trim the hair so the shaved area dips down to form a V-shaped bottom border.
3. Use scissors to very carefully cut off the hair from the edges of the ears, so that they come to a point at the top.

How to Choose a Groomer

Some people find the best thing about having a Yorkshire Terrier is the chance to brush their dogs' beautiful locks. These people keep their dogs in full-length coats, which need very little clipping. Most pet owners, however, find it's more convenient to keep their Yorkies in a companion clip. Because clipping requires more talent and practice than brushing, you should put some thought into deciding to whom to entrust your dog's safety, comfort, and coiffeur.

Most Yorkie owners prefer to have their dogs professionally groomed, for several reasons:

- Professional groomers will do a better job than you can, at least at first.
- Professional groomers are trained to notice abnormalities in your dog, such as lumps, anal sac problems, and ear problems, that you may miss.

BE PREPARED! Grooming Schedule

Coat	Long	Clipped
Combing	every 1–3 days	every 3–5 days
Bathing	weekly	every 2–3 weeks
Anus check and cleaning	daily	daily
Ear check	weekly	weekly
Eye cleaning	daily	daily
Nail trim	every 2–3 weeks	every 2–3 weeks
Tooth brushing	daily	daily
Professional grooming	optional (or monthly)	every 6–8 weeks

- Professional groomers can express anal sacs, which you probably don't want to do.
- Professional groomers can save you the expense of buying clippers and the time of grooming.

Of course, there are other reasons for preferring to do it yourself:

- Home grooming is less expensive after the initial investment.
- Home grooming doesn't require an appointment or car trip.
- Home grooming is easier on old dogs.
- Home grooming means you don't have to place your dog in somebody else's hands.

Checking out a groomer, and knowing what to look for, can help alleviate worries about your dog's safety and happiness. Ask friends with small dogs, especially Yorkies, who they use and what their experiences have been. Ask at your veterinary clinic. The clinic may have its own groomer, in which case you know the answer. And even if it doesn't, the staff may not want to make specific recommendations. But they might be able to tell you if they have heard complaints about specific groomers.

Still at a loss? Got to *www.findagroomer.com*.

Visit the grooming shop. Mid-morning is usually busiest, so you'll see them at their worst if you go then. Look for the following:

- Does the smell make you wretch? Of course it will smell like wet dog, but it shouldn't smell like urine or feces.
- Are any dogs treated roughly? Dogs may need to be handled firmly, as they're not always thrilled or cooperative, but they shouldn't be handled roughly.
- Are any dogs left unsupervised on the grooming table? A dog left with only his head in a neck loop could jump off the table and choke or

break his neck. On the other hand, if the dog has both a neck and rump loop, the groomer can step away from the table, but she should still keep him in sight.

- Are dogs left unsupervised in drying cages? Prefer a shop that fluff-dries its dogs, meaning they blow them dry by hand. If they do use cage driers, the driers absolutely must have timers that turn them off automatically, and the cages must be in sight of the groomer.

Ask what is covered in a grooming session. Typically, it's a bath, clip, blow-dry, and brush-out, along with toe-nail clip, ear cleaning, and, usually, anal sac expression and ear plucking. For Yorkies, a topknot or ponytail and bow are commonly included. Ask about the groomer's experience. Many good groomers belong to the National Dog Groomers Association, which is a good sign, but many other good groomers do not. Many have graduated from a grooming school, but many good groomers are self-taught or apprenticed under another groomer.

Once you've settled on a groomer, make an appointment and be honest about your dog's condition. The groomer will want to set aside the appropriate time in case your dog is extremely matted or needs extra work, rather than rushing through it. Expect to be charged more for excessive matting. In fact, talk to the groomer ahead of time and respect her judgment. It's often kindest to clip a heavily matted dog all the way down and start over, and it will probably save you money, too. Also be honest about your dog's behavior. Tell the groomer if he snaps when you try to cut his nails, or freaks out when the blow drier is turned on. The fewer surprises, the better for everyone, including your dog.

If your dog has no experience being clipped or groomed, don't expect miracles. The groomer may decide it's better not to fight over the small stuff, so you may not get the perfect clip you had in mind this first time. Dogs wriggle and jump, and you can't paste hair back on. Chances are, only another groomer would notice any imperfections. With experience, your dog will learn to take it all in stride, and his clips will reflect it. Occasionally, your dog will get a nick or rash, or a toenail will be cut too short. The groomer should inform you if that happens.

The Pedicure

An important part of your Yorkie's beauty treatment is actually also an important health precaution. Nails that grow too long can get caught in carpet loops and pulled from the nail bed, impacting the ground with every step, displacing the normal position of the toes, and causing discomfort, splaying, and even lameness. If dewclaws, those rudimentary "thumbs" on the wrists, are present, they are especially prone to getting caught on things and ripped out, and can even grow in a loop and back into the leg. They're easy to miss under all that hair! A groomer will clip your dog's nails, or you can have your veterinary clinic do it, but it's easier to do it yourself.

The best time to start is in puppyhood, so you can teach him early on that this is worth the treats you'll be heap on him for every nail cut. Do this enough, and avoid cutting the quick, and your Yorkie will be wishing he had more toes.

Use nail clippers—either the guillotine type or scissors type are fine for Yorkie nails. just be sure they are sharp, as dull clippers crush the nail and hurt. You can also use a tiny nail grinder, but don't let the heat build up, and don't let any long hair wrap around the shaft. The way to avoid this is by putting an old nylon stocking over the foot and pushing each nail through it before filing. You also have to make sure your Yorkie doesn't put his head near the grinder, where he could get his hair caught in it.

It's easiest to hold your Yorkie on his back in your lap to cut his nails. This allows you to see the quick, the sensitive and potentially bleeding part of the nail, better. If you look under the nail, you can see where it begins to get hollow; anywhere it looks hollow is quickless. In this same area, the

nail will suddenly get much thinner. Again, where it's thin, it's safe to cut. In a light-colored nail you can see a redder area that indicates the blood supply; the sensitive quick extends slightly further down the nail than the blood supply. When in doubt, cut too little and gradually whittle your way higher. You'll occasionally goof up and cut the quick. That calls for styptic powder to quell the bleeding and lots of extra treats to assuage your guilt!

Trimming the Feet

All Yorkies should have the hair between their footpads trimmed. Left long, it can cause the dog to slip and also attract dirt and debris, dispersing it around the house. You have to be very careful when trimming around the tiny paw pads, because they can be cut badly by a powerful clipper. It's safer to use a moustache trimmer or small, blunt-nosed scissors. Dogs tend to be ticklish there, so be prepared for jumpy paws.

Start by trimming the edge along the outside of the foot, so the hair doesn't reach the ground but instead forms a rounded edge. Then carefully trim the hair from under the foot, between the pads.

Chapter Nine

The Senior Yorkshire Terrier

Yorkshire Terriers have the gift of longevity. Barring unforeseen illness or accidents, most can live well into their teens, and the late teens are not out of the question. A few Yorkies have even lived into their twenties! One key to living to old age is having the good fortune to have good genes, but another key is having the good fortune to have good care.

Yorkie puppies are adorable, and Yorkie adults are fun. But Yorkie seniors, with the wisdom of their years, are in many ways the best Yorkies of all. You may need to make some concessions, of course, to help them be healthy and comfortable, but the extra effort you make will be well worth it.

Home Care

Younger Yorkies tend to treat your home like their personal circus, leaping on and off furniture in daredevil stunts. Older Yorkies may develop arthritic changes that can be made worse by such leaps. It may take them a while to realize that they should avoid wild leaps, but you can encourage them to instead use doggy steps or a ramp to get on beds and sofas.

Arthritic changes may also mean you can't take your Yorkie on marathon walks, or run him until exhaustion as you used to. Although he still needs exercise, it should be low-impact exercise like walking, and not to the point that he's exhausted the rest of the day. If he has difficulty getting up and moving around the next day, you may have overdone it.

Just because his body may be slowing, it doesn't mean his mind is. He still needs mental stimulation. If he enjoys the same games he did when he was younger, great! Just be sure not to overdo them. He may prefer less-strenuous activities, though. Hide treats around the room and challenge him to find them. Take him for rides in the car, strolls in a doggy stroller or in a doggy purse, or just short walks where he mostly just sniffs around.

But be careful. Older dogs are more susceptible to both chills and overheating, so be sure to keep an eye on whether he's curled up and shivering or spread out and panting. Vacation plans should take his needs into

consideration. Long trips can be grueling for an older dog, but boarding can be even more stressful. Weigh carefully the pros and cons of each before deciding what to do with your vacation time.

Feeding

More than 40 percent of dogs between the ages of 5 and 10 years are overweight or obese. And it's not just from less activity or more eating. Changes in metabolic rate cause fewer calories to be burned, and more to be stored as fat. A recent study showed that mature dogs require 20 percent fewer calories in order to maintain the same weight as younger ones. Dogs entering old age may benefit from eating a food with less fat and fewer calories.

But there's a catch when it comes to very old dogs. As dogs continue to age they tend to stop gaining weight and instead start losing weight, actually requiring more calories. For these dogs, increasing the fat content of the diet will increase tastiness and calorie content, and also improve protein efficiency.

Older dogs may have different protein requirements. Even with exercise, older dogs tend to lose muscle mass, which means losses in protein reserves. Losses in muscle tissue and protein reserves may impair the immune system and decrease the body's ability to respond to physical trauma, infectious agents, or stress. Older dogs need higher levels of dietary protein to build and maintain muscle and counteract these potential problems. Contrary to popular opinion, feeding older dogs a high-protein diet will not overtax their kidneys—unless the dog already has kidney problems. Dogs with kidney problems need to eat a diet with moderate levels of high-quality protein; however, older dogs without kidney disease can eat a high-protein diet without adverse kidney effects.

In most healthy older dogs, dietary mineral levels can remain the same. For example, sodium restriction is not necessary. However, many older dogs are hypertensive or have heart disease. Not only is excess sodium bad for these conditions, but the conditions may also make it difficult to excrete excess sodium in the diet. Most diets supply more sodium than is required, so decreasing sodium is usually a good idea as long as the dog will still eat his food.

Unlike people, dogs don't seem to suffer from osteoporosis, at least not if they've been maintained on a balanced diet with adequate calcium in earlier years. Thus, senior dogs eating a commercial diet do not need calcium supplementation.

Don't forget the practical aspects. Old dogs are more prone to dehydration, often because of health problems such as kidney disease that cause them to urinate more frequently, or because they're taking medications such as diuretics for heart disease. Making sure his water is fresh, cool, and readily available can help encourage a dog to drink more.

Helpful Hints

Eat!

It doesn't matter what's in the bowl if your dog won't eat it. Because oral disease is the most common problem for older Yorkies, some dogs may find overly large or hard kibble or biscuits uncomfortable to chew. A blunted sense of smell, or concurrent disease or some medications, may also cause older dogs to have less appetite. Try serving warmed or soft foods. You may have to hand-feed him. Remember, the best food is the one your senior Yorkie will actually eat, even if the label isn't perfect.

Grooming

If you have made a habit of regularly grooming your Yorkie's long tresses throughout his life, he may look forward to his grooming sessions as a relaxing time. However, if it's been a battle all these years, consider clipping him down if you haven't already done so. If he's uneasy at the groomer, learn to clip him yourself. It's not that difficult. Another option is to have a groomer come to your home to groom, or find one who makes appointments and can groom while you wait, rather than have him stay all day. Most groomers will be considerate of their older dogs' needs.

Don't forget the toenails! Older dogs have tougher nails, and they wear them down less. They can grow to the point that it makes walking difficult.

It's not uncommon for older dogs to have a stronger body odor than they did when younger. Search for its source. The most likely sources are the teeth, ear infections, seborrhea (dandruff), and even kidney disease.

Senior Health

Your older Yorkie should have a veterinary checkup twice a year. Whereas bloodwork may have been optional when he was younger, it's a necessity now. It can tell you if he has kidney failure, diabetes, liver failure, or other problems.

Because the immune system is less effective in older dogs, it's doubly important for you to shield your Yorkie from infectious disease, However, if he's turned into a homebody, it may not be necessary for him to continue being vaccinated. This is an area of controversy. Ask your veterinarian about the latest guidelines.

Vomiting and diarrhea can dehydrate and debilitate an old dog quickly. They can also signal some possibly serious problems. So while you may have waited a bit when he was younger, you can't afford to wait and see when it comes to your older Yorkie.

Breed Truths

Dental Problems

Tooth problems are very common in older Yorkies. Bad breath, lip licking, reluctance to chew, or avoidance of hands near his mouth are all signs that your dog needs veterinary dental attention. Pulling loose teeth and cleaning the remaining teeth can help your dog feel much better.

Many disorders that are rare in young dogs are not uncommon in old dogs. Heart disease, kidney disease, cancer, diabetes, and Cushing's syndrome are all much more common in older dogs. Symptoms of these disorders include diarrhea, coughing, appetite changes, weight loss, abdominal distension, and increased thirst and urination. Many of these disorders can be treated successfully, especially if caught early.

Senior Changes

Older dogs, like older people, may experience sensory or cognitive losses. Fortunately, dogs deal well with these changes—better, in fact, than most people do.

Vision loss. As your dog ages, you'll start to notice a slight haziness when you look into the pupil (the black part) of his eye. That's normal, and it doesn't affect vision that much. However, if it becomes very gray or even white, he probably has cataracts. A canine ophthalmologist can remove the lens and even replace it with an artificial lens, just like people get.

Hearing loss. Older dogs also tend to lose their hearing. The ability to hear high-pitched sounds usually goes first, so try to call out in a lower tone of voice. Dogs can easily learn hand signals, and they can also learn to come to a flashing porch light when out in the yard. Be sure to pet your dog a lot; otherwise he might wonder why you've quit talking to him.

Cognitive loss. If you find your older Yorkie walking around aimlessly, pacing back and forth, or standing in a corner looking like he's stuck, he may be suffering from cognitive dysfunction. Basically, he's having a hard

time thinking as clearly as he once did. Your veterinarian can prescribe drugs that may help him back to being his old self. You can also help by involving him in activities and small mental challenges, either through games or by teaching him new tricks. These have been shown to help ward off cognitive impairment.

Arthritis. Older dogs often suffer from arthritis, in which the joints become stiff and painful. You can help your arthritic dog by walking him a short distance one or more times a day. Ask your veterinarian about drugs that may help alleviate some of the symptoms, or even improve the joint.

Helpful Hints

Living With a Blind Yorkie

If your Yorkie loses his vision, block dangerous places, such as stairways and pools. Don't move your furniture. Place sound and scent beacons around the house and yard so he can hear and smell where he is. Make pathways, such as carpet runners inside and gravel walks outside, that he can feel with his paws.

167

Chapter Ten

The Yorkshire Terrier Standard

The ideal Yorkshire Terrier in your eyes is probably the one that looks just like the one in your lap. But the ideal Yorkshire Terrier in the eyes of an impartial judge has to be evaluated by means of the Yorkshire Terrier standard of perfection, which describes exactly how the dog should look.

The following is an encapsulation of the highlights of the AKC Yorkshire Terrier breed standard. Of greatest importance is the general appearance, which is described as follows:

> "That of a long-haired toy terrier whose blue-and-tan coat is parted on the face and from the base of the skull to the end of the tail and hangs evenly and quite straight down each side of body. The body is neat, compact and well proportioned. The dog's high head carriage and confident manner should give the appearance of vigor and self importance."

Weight: Must not exceed 7 pounds.

Coat: The Yorkshire Terrier's coat is of prime importance, so the standard devotes a lot of attention to it. Hair is glossy, fine, and silky in texture. Coat on the body is moderately long and perfectly straight (not wavy). It may be trimmed to floor length to give ease of movement and a neater appearance, if desired. The fall on the head is long, tied with one bow in center of head or parted in the middle and tied with two bows. The hair on muzzle is very long. Hair should be trimmed short on tips of ears and may be trimmed on feet to give them a neat appearance.

Color: Puppies are born black and tan and are normally darker in body color, showing an intermingling of black hair in the tan until they are matured. Color of hair on body and richness of tan on head and legs are of prime importance in adult dogs, to which the following color requirements apply:

- Blue: A dark steel blue, not a silver blue and not mingled with fawn, bronzy, or black hairs.
- Tan: Darker at the roots than in the middle, shading to still lighter tan at the tips. There should be no sooty or black hair intermingled with any of the tan.

Color on body: The blue extends over the body from back of neck to root of tail. Hair on tail is a darker blue, especially at end of tail.

Head fall color: A rich golden tan, deeper in color at sides of head, at ear roots, and on the muzzle, with ears a deep, rich tan. Tan color should not extend down on back of neck.

Chest and leg color: A bright, rich tan, not extending above the elbow on the forelegs nor above the stifle on the hind legs.

Breed Truths

Judging the Yorkshire Terrier

For more information about interpreting the Yorkie standard, visit

www.ytca.org/education1.html or *www.yorkiebaby.com/judge.html*

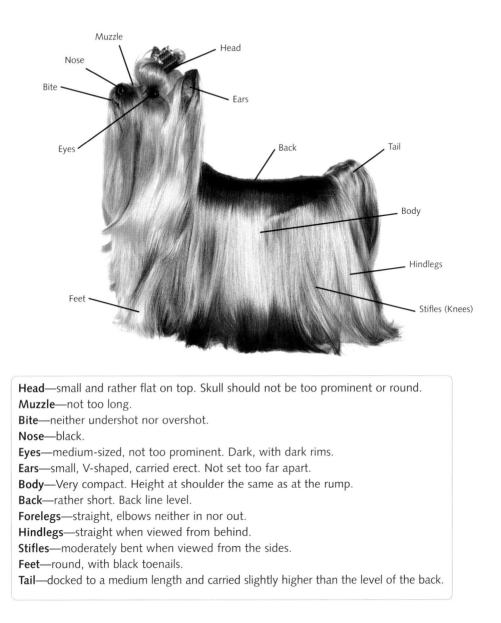

Head—small and rather flat on top. Skull should not be too prominent or round.
Muzzle—not too long.
Bite—neither undershot nor overshot.
Nose—black.
Eyes—medium-sized, not too prominent. Dark, with dark rims.
Ears—small, V-shaped, carried erect. Not set too far apart.
Body—Very compact. Height at shoulder the same as at the rump.
Back—rather short. Back line level.
Forelegs—straight, elbows neither in nor out.
Hindlegs—straight when viewed from behind.
Stifles—moderately bent when viewed from the sides.
Feet—round, with black toenails.
Tail—docked to a medium length and carried slightly higher than the level of the back.

Disqualification: Any solid color or combination of colors other than blue and tan as described above. Any white markings other than a small white spot on the forechest that does not exceed 1 inch at its longest dimension. Note: Immature dogs not having a totally clear tan or immature dogs that are not yet totally blue are acceptable under the breed standard and should not be disqualified. The Yorkshire Terrier has a slow metamorphosis from the black-and-tan puppy to the blue-and-tan adult, some taking three or more years.

Resources

All-Breed Organizations

American Kennel Club (AKC)
www.akc.org

Canadian Kennel Club
www.ckc.ca

United Kennel Club (UKC)
www.ukcdogs.com

Yorkshire Terrier Organizations

Yorkshire Terrier Club of America (YTCA)
www.ytca.org

Regional Yorkshire Terrier Clubs
www.ytca.org/regionalclubs.html

YTCA Breeder Contacts
www.ytca.org/breeder1.html

Sweety Blue ("The King of Yorkshire Terrier Sites")
www.sweetyblue.com

Henceforths Yorkie News
www.henceforths.com

Working Yorkies
www.geocities.com/workingyorkie

Yorkie Club
www.yorkieclub.com

Yorkshire Terrier Journal
www.yorkshire-terrier-journal.com

Rescue Organizations

See page 25

Health Information and Research

AKC Canine Health Foundation
www.akcchf.org

Canine Eye Registration Foundation
www.vmdb.org

Canine Health Information Center
www.caninehealthinfo.org

Morris Animal Foundation
www.morrisanimalfoundation.org

National Animal Poison Control Center
(800) 548-2423
www.napcc.aspca.org

Optigen (DNA testing for progressive renal atrophy)
www.optigen.com

Orthopedic Foundation for Animals
www.offa.org

YTCA Foundation
www.yorkiefoundation.org

Index

THE TEAM BEHIND THE *TRAIN YOUR DOG* DVD

Host **Nicole Wilde** is a certified Pet Dog Trainer and internationally recognized author and lecturer. Her books include *So You Want to be a Dog Trainer* and *Help for Your Fearful Dog* (Phantom Publishing). In addition to working with dogs, Nicole has been working with wolves and wolf hybrids for over fifteen years and is considered an expert in the field.

Host **Laura Bourhenne** is a Professional Member of the Association of Pet Dog Trainers, and holds a degree in Exotic Animal Training. She has trained many species of animals including several species of primates, birds of prey, and many more. Laura is striving to enrich the lives of pets by training and educating the people they live with.

Director **Leo Zahn** is an award winning director/cinematographer/editor of television commercials, movies, and documentaries. He has directed and edited more than a dozen instructional DVDs through the Picture Company, a subsidiary of Picture Palace, Inc., based in Los Angeles.